P9-BZP-121

Earl Thollander's
Back Roads of California

Store and Post Office,
Plumas County

ASAHI BEER

THE BIG TREES BOTTLING CO.
BLOOSER
BIER
SAN FRANCISCO USA

WARNING · DEPT. OF
HEALTH SAYS BLOOSER
IS HARMLESS IF
LEFT IN THE BOTTLE

Coke

A. RUBE'S TOOLS

OREDAZAC ORACLE
~ NOTHING ~
ABSOLUTELY NOTHING
EVER HAPPENED HERE UNTIL THE YEAR 1871.
A. RUBE LOST HIS WAGONLOAD OF SUPPLIES
THAT HE WAS BRINGING FROM PETALUMA WHEN
HE ATTEMPTED TO FORD AUSTIN CREEK AT THIS SPOT.
FLOUR, BEER, COFFEE, BACON, BEANS, POWDER, JEANS
AND TOOLS ALL HAD TO BE AGAIN BROUGHT FROM
PORT PETALUMA TO SUPPLY HIS FAMILY NEEDS.

NOTHING, ABSOLUTELY NOTHING ELSE HAPPENED
HERE UNTIL THE YEAR OF ECOLOGY
1971 WHEN THIS MEMORIAL WAS ERECTED
AS THE LAST RESTING PLACE OF THESE
BOTTLES OF
NO ~ RETURN

Folk art sketched near Cazadero (Oredazac spelled backward), Sonoma County

Earl Thollander's
Back Roads of California

Clarkson N. Potter, Inc./Publishers NEW YORK

DISTRIBUTED BY CROWN PUBLISHERS, INC.

to dear friends
Bill and Barbara

Copyright © 1983 by Earl Thollander

All rights reserved. No part of this book may be reproduced or transmitted in any form or by any means, electronic or mechanical, including photocopying, recording, or by any information storage and retrieval system, without permission in writing from the publisher.

Published by Clarkson N. Potter, Inc., 225 Park Avenue South, New York, New York 10003 and represented in Canada by the Canadian MANDA Group

Manufactured in the United States of America

Library of Congress Cataloging-in-Publication Data

Thollander, Earl.
    Earl Thollander's back roads of California.

    1. California—Description and travel—1981—Guide-books.   2. Automobiles—Road guides—California.
I. Title.   II. Title: Back roads of California.
F859.3.T525   1983   917.94'0453   82-22461
ISBN 0-517-54966-2 (cloth)
ISBN 0-517-54967-0 (paper)

10 9 8 7 6 5 4 3

Bush Penstemon, Santa Clara County

Contents

Rural mailbox,
Knoxville Road, Napa County

Central California

Map legend

.___5.6___. distance in miles between dots

→ → → my route (which may be reversed should you desire)

▲ campgrounds
■ towns and cities
▭ dams
--- lake boundaries
-..- trails
.... rivers
▢ special place
✕ my sketching place
⌂ church
π picnic grounds
⊞ cemetery
△ mountains
⌂ buildings

NORTH is always toward the top of the page

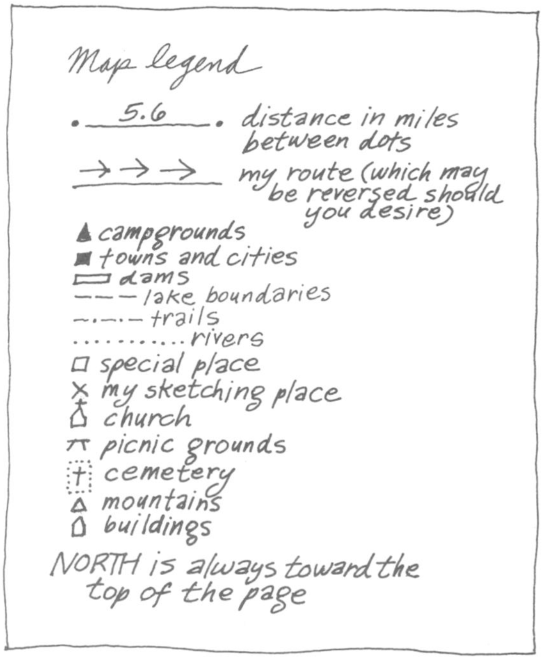

p. napa county

I am grateful to the artist Joe Seney for his good companionship on many of these back road journeys.

Turkey Buzzard,
Stanislaus County

Preface

Earl Thollander's Back Roads of California is a nonhighway travel guide to out of the way places. A sequel to the first Back Roads of California published more than a decade ago, this new volume augments it to make a more complete guide to areas throughout California. The trips included are as beautiful and as interesting as those in the first volume.

Each of the book's four parts begins with a sectional map. These will help you locate the back roads on larger maps that are available from many sources, including travel services, chambers of commerce, gas stations, tourist bureaus, and automobile clubs.

Localized maps for all roads throughout the book will guide you on specific trips. Arrows trace my direction of travel, although the routes can easily be reversed. The North Pole is toward the top of the page. Maps are not to scale because the roads are of varying lengths; however, the mileage notations will provide a sense of their distance.

Your odometer will not measure distance exactly the same as mine, but the differences should not be too great. AAA county and regional maps were essential to me in following the back roads. I also purchased maps at ranger stations when entering forest preserves.

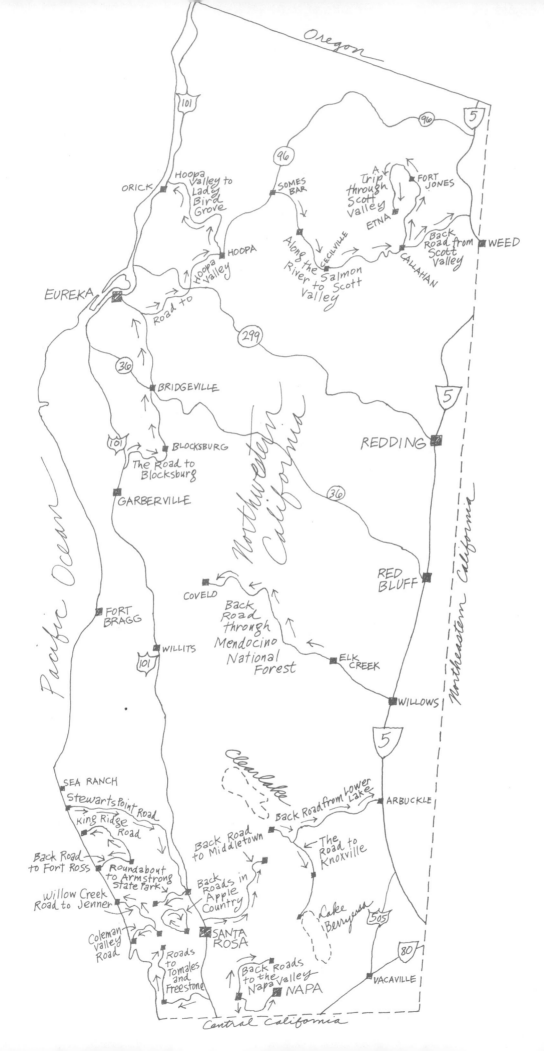

I've heard people boast of how fast they went somewhere and how many miles were covered in the time. In the pages that follow there are mountain and coastal roads to enjoy with no regard for speed or the hour.

I start early and let the day unfold. I don't push to get anywhere because I know that the fun and beauty of the back road experience is in the trip itself.

I hesitate to divulge certain roads, but it would be unrealistic to believe they can be saved from change by hiding them. Only for a while, perhaps. And, of course, they are not secret. They are public roads and are catalogued on county maps. Better to announce their charm and beauty and alert everyone interested to guard against infringements upon them. I also like to think that back road travelers like myself will not drop trash or create disturbances along the way.

Those who live on the back roads and we who enjoy traveling them must be concerned that they remain unspoiled as long as possible.

California Poppy, Tehama County

Roads to Tomales and Freestone

Rolling pastureland, cows, old farms, leaning barns, and rows of eucalyptus distinguish this area of California.   I sketch along Carmody Road with a meadowlark's song in the still morning air.
Curious cows peer at me, then go back to munching the green grass.
The village of Tomales was established at the head of Keyes Creek with the opening of a store there in 1852. Tomales made its first rail shipment of produce to Sausalito — via the North Pacific Coast Railroad — in 1874, when 300 sacks of potatoes were delivered to be ferried across the Golden Gate to San Francisco.

The view from Carmody Road, Marin and Sonoma counties

14

I sketch the town from across the hills, then drive to nearby Dillon Beach overlooking Bodega Bay. The bay was named by its discoverer, Juan Francisco de la Bodega y Cuadro, in 1775.

The village of Tomales, Marin County

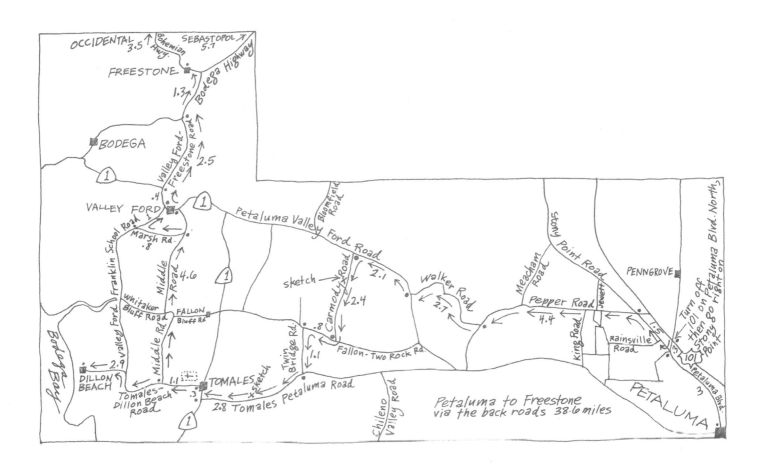

Back roads bring me to Freestone. The
town derived its name from a kind of easily
worked, or free, sandstone quarry nearby.
I sketch the old, restored hilltop schoolhouse.
The original railroad hostelry, known as Hinds Hotel
in 1873, is still there, today called Freestone
House.   I also investigate the interesting plant
nursery and zoo.

Old schoolhouse at Freestone, Sonoma County

Coleman Valley Road to the sea

I begin a journey to the coast on Coleman Valley Road off Occidental town's Third Street. The road winds through hilly meadow and forest. Trees are less in evidence as I approach the coast and sheep roam the smooth green hillsides. The road becomes a ridge route with views all around. Fields of low-growing purple iris are in bloom in the spring landscape. Deep green ravines and rows of coastal mountains carry the eye further and further until the sea comes into view. On the ridge above the ocean I sketch the old Irish Hill Ranch, originally owned by the Fitzgeralds. I hear that the ranch owners switched from cows to sheep farming during the Second World War because the lights required for early milkings were banned by wartime coastal blackout controls. It was easier to raise sheep than to lightproof a big, old barn or milk a whole herd of cows in the dark.

From Irish Hill to the sea

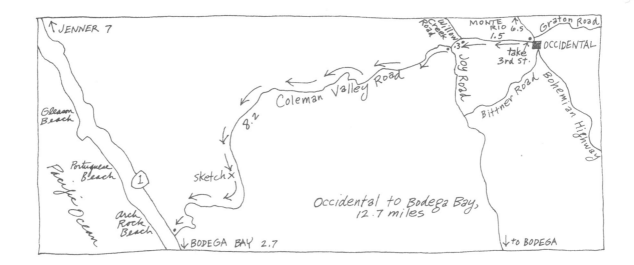

↑ JENNER 7

Gleason Beach

Portuguese Beach

Pacific Ocean

1

Arch Rock Beach

sketch X

8.2

Coleman Valley Road

↓ BODEGA BAY 2.7

Willow Creek Road

.3

MONTE RIO 6.5

Graton Road

take 3rd St.

OCCIDENTAL

Joy Road

Bittner Road

Bohemian Highway

Occidental to Bodega Bay, 12.7 miles

↓ to BODEGA

20

Willow Creek Road to Jenner

From the end of Occidental's hilly Third Street, I sketch the historic Union Hotel, where in the late 1800s dances attracted revelers from Bodega, Freestone, Valley Ford, Sebastopol, and even Santa Rosa. The "highest railroad bridge west of the Mississippi was located near here at the time. It was said of the early town, "It lies in the heart of a redwood forest, and the old stumps still stand in the streets." Evidence of early Italian settlement is still apparent with the flourishing of Neapolitan restaurants in town.

Also pictured in my drawing is the 1903 Church of St. Philip.

Occidental, Sonoma County

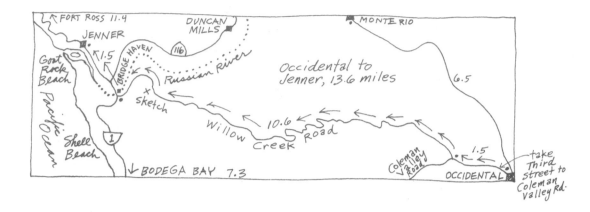

I drive the partly unpaved route to Jenner along Willow Creek Road. It is winding and heavily forested at times. Cattle chew their cuds and swat flies with their tails as they lounge among big ferns in the shade of a redwood grove. A hawk and a raven swoop and clash with each other in the sky above.

I draw a farmhouse nestled in a valley near the coast where Willow Creek flows into the Russian River.

Willow Creek farm, Sonoma County

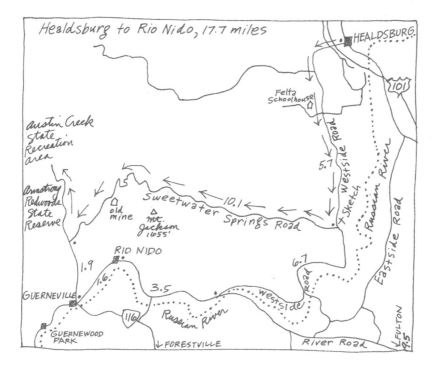

Sweetwater landscape, Sonoma County

Roundabout to Armstrong State Park

Westside Road gives views of lush farm country and the thick green of grapevines growing in the summer sun. At Sweetwater Springs turnoff, I sketch a view of a triple-stack hop kiln with Mt. St. Helena in the distance.

Healdsburg to Rio Nido, 17.7 miles

HEALDSBURG

Felta Schoolhouse

101

Austin Creek State Recreation area

5.7 Westside Road

Russian River

Armstrong Redwoods State Reserve

old mine

mt. Jackson 1655'

Sweetwater Springs Road

10.1

X Sketch

Eastside Road

RIO NIDO

6.7

1.9

1.6

3.5

GUERNEVILLE

116

Westside Road

Russian River

L. Fulton 9.5

GUERNEWOOD PARK

↓ FORESTVILLE

River Road

Hops, used as flavoring for beer, were a major crop in
this area at one time. The long vines were hung to dry
in these decorative buildings. The hop kilns are now
used for a winery.

Sweetwater Springs Road has a primitive feel to it.
Skirting Mount Jackson, it undoubtedly was made with a great
deal of effort by early road builders. It twists and turns
and is a bit steep and narrow—a more adventurous trip
than merely continuing around the mountain on Westside
Road. For those wishing an effortless, yet scenic route
to Armstrong State Park, stay on Westside.

At Armstrong, ancient live redwoods may be viewed.

Back road to Fort Ross

From the wooded hamlet of Cazadero, Fort Ross Road winds up and over the coastal mountains. A fire had charred the landscape a few years back; however, the slow regeneration of the forest is now in process. Burned redwoods are striking new branches and seedling firs are sprouting new spring needles. Closer to the sea, purple iris blooms in quantity. At Fort Ross, a brisk, cool breeze blows across the bluffs where I choose to sketch.

Fort Ross, Sonoma County

Fine restoration has been done on the old Russian fort.
In 1834 the Chief Ruler of the Russian Colonies in America
had described it like this: "There have been erected two
towers with cannons defending all sides of this so-called
fort, which appears to the eyes of the Indians and
local Spaniards, however, as being very strong and
possibly even unconquerable. Within the enclosure...
stand...the home of the director..., barracks, stores,
and a chapel, kept in cleanliness and order... outside the
fort... are located two company cattle barns, spacious and
distinctively clean, with pens, a small building for
storing milk and making butter, a shed for the Indians, a
threshing floor, and two rows of small company and private
homes with gardens and orchards.... In a clearing...stands a
windmill...at a wharf for canoes are a broad shed and
trading station, a blacksmithery, a tannery, and a bath house."

Back road sign,
Napa County

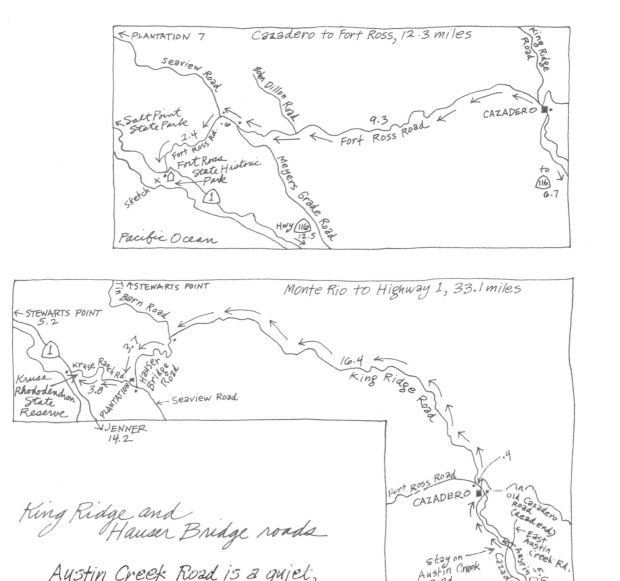

King Ridge and
Hauser Bridge roads

Austin Creek Road is a quiet,
leisurely back road to Cazadero.
There are lots of redwood
trees, and houses snuggle in
deep shade to the creek edge.
Along King Ridge Road out
of Cazadero, long views of the coastal mountain
chain are outlined. It is grazing land and the
road winds like an old cattle trail, skirting ancient
wooden fencing and traversing the crests of dun-
colored mountaintops. Hauser Bridge Road then
dips down to where a narrow steel bridge crosses
the picturesque Gualala River, then up and over
another ridge and down to Plantation.
        Plantation had a post office and a
hotel in earlier days; it is now a private children's camp.
As I sketch the Plantation barn, several cars emerge
     from Kruse Rhododendron State Reserve, their
occupants stopping to ask, "Where am I" and "Where
         are the rhododendrons?"

The rhododendron's rose-tinted blooms appear between March and June. (This was a hot July day.) I proceed through the Reserve after leaving Plantation and note great clumps of rhododendrons disguised as green leaves at this time of year. The red-woods had been logged in the 1890s, and in the 1000-year cycle it takes to return to a redwood forest, the tanbark oak and rhododendron stage has been reached. Some tanbarks have been removed to keep from smothering out the colorful rhododendrons.

The white barn, Plantation, Sonoma County

The store at Stewarts Point, Sonoma County

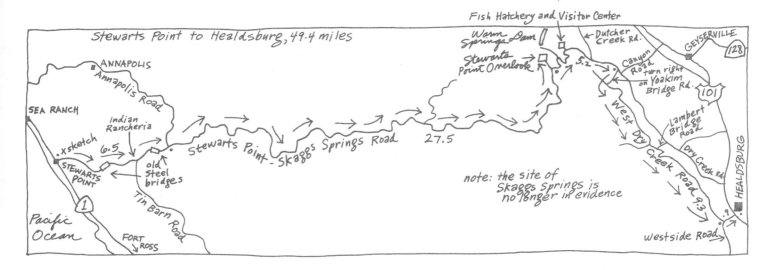

The Stewarts Point - Skaggs Springs Road

Opposite the quaint 1868 Stewarts Point store, the Stewarts Point-Skaggs Springs Road ascends through dense fir and redwood forest. An old steel bridge spans the Gualala River. I remember hoping that it wouldn't soon be replaced with the usual uninteresting modern concrete crossing. There is access to the river here and a possible picnicking spot.

I view ranges of coastal mountains as the road winds up and over various summits. Skaggs Springs was at one time a celebrated watering place which, in the 1860s, could accommodate 300 people. A writer of the time gave this description of the Springs: "There are here a few acres of tolerable, level fertile land; the rest of the country is pretty slanting; in fact up edgeways, and they pasture goats on both sides of it. There are plenty of deer in the vicinity, but it is very dangerous hunting them; if you should kill one it would be liable to fall on your head."

The road eventually becomes wider and faster as I approach the Warm Springs Dam area. The Stewarts Point Overlook affords a dramatic view of the dam. I take West Dry Creek Road down a narrow valley planted with grapevines and plum trees to Highway 101 and Healdsburg.

Back roads in apple country

Apple orchards pattern the up-and-down hills west of Sebastopol, although new housing and new vineyards have downed a number of trees in this picturesque countryside.

apples near Sebastopol, Sonoma County

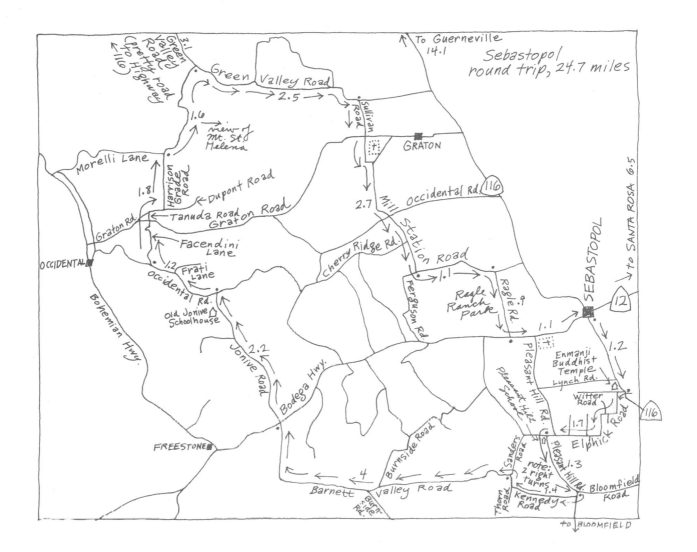

The main town, Sebastopol, was named for the Crimean port
 in the USSR. In the late 1800s it was famous as the
birthplace of canned applesauce. An architectural
 tour of Sebastopol has been published by the Western
 Sonoma Historical Society, P.O. Box 816, Sebastopol.
It includes a temple, which had traveled in toto from
 Japan to the Chicago World's Fair (1933-34) and then
 home to Sebastopol.
   The rolling hills and winding roads take me
through a varied landscape —— from apple-growing areas
 to deep valleys and meadows. Apple trees give way
to oaks and eucalyptus. Along Jonive Road are firs and
 redwoods and on Harrison Grade I drive past juniper
 and manzanita before returning to apple country and Sebastopol.

Back roads to the Napa Valley

In the deep shade of its garden I sketch Lachryma Montis (Tears of the Mountain), once the home of General Mariano Guadalupe Vallejo. It was named for the spring that supplied water to both the farm and the early town of Sonoma. In town I stop at the Sonoma League for Historic Preservation, 129 East Spain, to pick up its good walking guide to the town.

I travel the back roads from here into Napa County's Carneros district. Here, near the upper reaches of San Francisco Bay, the climate is cooler. It is a good place to plant wine grapes of the early maturing variety.

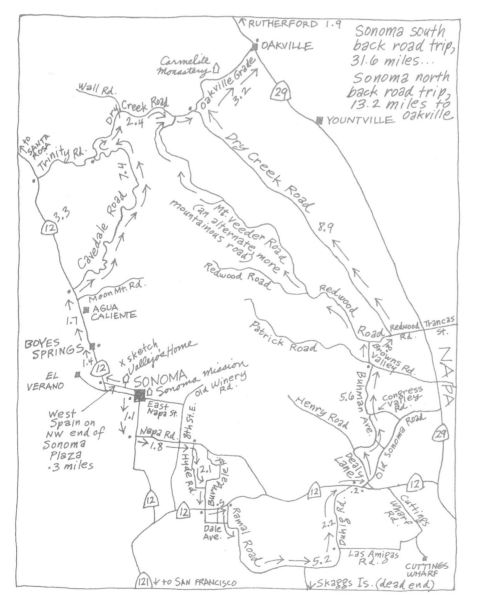

Sonoma south back road trip, 31.6 miles...

Sonoma north back road trip, 13.2 miles to Oakville

North of Sonoma, I look for Cavedale Road. It winds up into the Mayacamas Range with good views of Sonoma Valley. Toyon, maple, madrone, oak, bay, and fir trees seem to close in over the road. Joining Trinity Road, I travel over the mountains toward Oakville, stopping to enjoy an expansive view of Napa Valley.

Lachryma Montis, Sonoma County

Back road to Middletown

I pass Mark West Springs, where mineral hot springs were discovered in 1857. It had become a popular spa in the 19th century, famous for its sulphur baths. Ancient grapevines twine over the road at this point.

Franz Valley Road winds over the crest of the Mayacamas Range and drops into Franz Valley with a distant view of Mount St. Helena.

I reach Knight's Valley, named for Thomas Knight who came to California in 1845. By 1853 Knight had earned enough money, possibly in gold mining, to purchase a large portion of the fertile valley and become a farmer.

Ida Clayton Road, circling the western side of Mount St. Helena brings me to the view I sketch. This was a mining road in the 1860s.

Massive and majestic, Mt. St. Helena, at 4,343 feet, rises almost twice as high as surrounding mountains. Probably a fable, it has been written that it was named by Helena de Gagarin, wife of the Governor-General of the Russian colonies in America. On June 20, 1841, she headed an expedition that ascended the mountain. At the top she christened it St. Helena in honor of the patron saint of the Empress of Russia.

Mt. St. Helena,
Sonoma County

39

Back road to Middletown

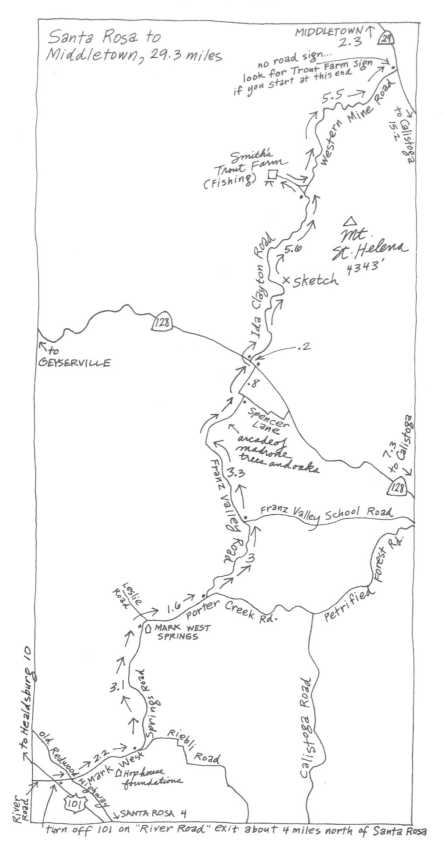

Santa Rosa to Middletown, 29.3 miles

MIDDLETOWN ↑ 2.3 — 29

no road sign... look for Trout Farm sign if you start at this end

5.5 →

Western Mine Road

to Calistoga 15.2

Smith's Trout Farm (Fishing)

Mt. St. Helena 4343'

5.6

× sketch

Ida Clayton Road

128

← to GEYSERVILLE

.2

.8

Spencer Lane

arcade of madrone trees and oaks

7.3 to Calistoga

128

Franz Valley Road

3.3

Franz Valley School Road

Petrified Forest Rd.

3

Leslie Road

1.6 →

Porter Creek Rd.

Calistoga Road

□ MARK WEST SPRINGS

Springs Road

3.1

Riebli Road

old Redwood Highway

to Healdsburg 10

2.2

Mark West

□ Hop house foundations

River Road

101

SANTA ROSA 4 ↓

turn off 101 on "River Road" exit about 4 miles north of Santa Rosa

40

Lower Lake back road and the road to Knoxville

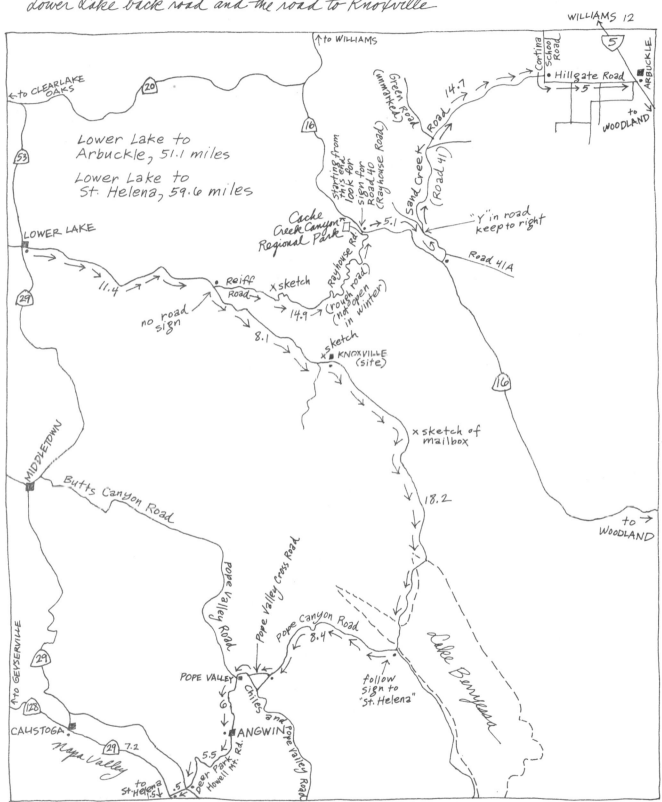

↑ to WILLIAMS

WILLIAMS 12

to CLEARLAKE OAKS ←

20

16

53

Lower Lake to
Arbuckle, 51.1 miles

Lower Lake to
St. Helena, 59.6 miles

Cortina
School Road

Hillgate Road

ARBUCKLE

5

14.7

to WOODLAND

Green Road
(unmarked)
(Rayhouse Road)

Sand Creek

Road 14.7

(Road 41)

Starting from this end look for sign for Road 40 (Rayhouse Road)

Cache Creek Canyon Regional Park

5.1

"y" in road keep to right

5

Road 41A

LOWER LAKE

29

11.4

Reiff Road

X sketch

Rayhouse Rd.

no road sign

14.9 →

(rough road) (not open in winter)

8.1

X sketch

KNOXVILLE (site)

16

X sketch of mailbox

MIDDLETOWN

Butts Canyon Road

18.2

to WOODLAND

to GEYSERVILLE

29

Pope Valley Road

Pope Valley Cross Road

Pope Canyon Road

8.4

Lake Berryessa

follow sign to "St. Helena"

128

POPE VALLEY

Chiles and Pope Valley Road

6

CALISTOGA

29   7.2

ANGWIN

5.5

Deer Park Howell Mt. Rd.

Napa Valley

to St. Helena ↓   .5   .5   .4

Back road from Lower Lake

Lower Lake has a colorful mining town look to it. The 1868 IOOF building and the old jail still stand, as does the bulky brick 1877 schoolhouse with its second-story dance hall.

Morgan Valley Road heads east from here through farm country and into steeper hills where blue-green oaks and black-barked serpentine pines predominate.

Unmarked, Reiff Road goes east into Yolo County through the Blue Ridge Mountains to Highway 16 and Cache Creek Regional Park. I stop at the Reiff Ranch to sketch a barn built by the family in 1930. Mr. Reiff talks of fixing the structure because the mudsills, which had been its foundation, are gone and barn supports have gone askew. We agree that all a well-built barn needs is good roofing and a proper foundation and it will last forever. The road from here to Highway 16 bumps and joggles. It is a slow-going back road (and "closed during winter," a sign reports). I pass old, rusty mining buildings and, at another point, enjoy dramatic views of rugged mountains. Road 41 (Sand Creek Road) affords scenic views of the fertile valley far below. And, on topping the ridge, a view of mountains and hills, superimposed one on the next, extends as far as the eye can see.

Reiff Barn,
Lake County

43

The road to Knoxville (map, page 41)

In July grassy slopes shimmer with soft, golden light. Groves of oak trees make blue-green silhouettes on the hillsides and canyons.

At Knoxville I sketch the ghostly Manhattan Quicksilver Mine Headquarters building. Several 14-inch, spotted, black and tan alligator lizards eye me at close range and I shoo off the fierce-looking creatures with my drawing pad. Unusually curious, they return again and again, enjoying my little game.

South of Knoxville, Lake Berryessa gleams bright blue contrasting with the surrounding dun-colored hills.

Manhattan Quicksilver Mine Office, Knoxville, Napa County

Round Valley Church, Covelo, Mendocino County

46

Back road through Mendocino National Forest

This forest was conserved for the nation by President Theodore Roosevelt in 1907. Highway 162 from Willows continues just a few miles north of Elk Creek, climbing high into brush-covered mountains. I stopped to look at Grindstone Canyon and read a forest service sign pointing out brush clearance projects. Grass is planted for the deer and cow populations, instead of allowing brush to proliferate.

Up higher I am in a vast conifer forest with views of adjoining mountain ranges. As I proceed further the land opens up with more grazing areas. Views are often magnificent.

I reach Covelo in Round Valley and draw the Methodist Church. A squirrel looks out of the faded pink and white bell tower while woodpeckers fly back and forth adding new acorn holes to it. A poster in the church entrance announces that in a few days the church will host a free movie, "The Horror of Dracula."

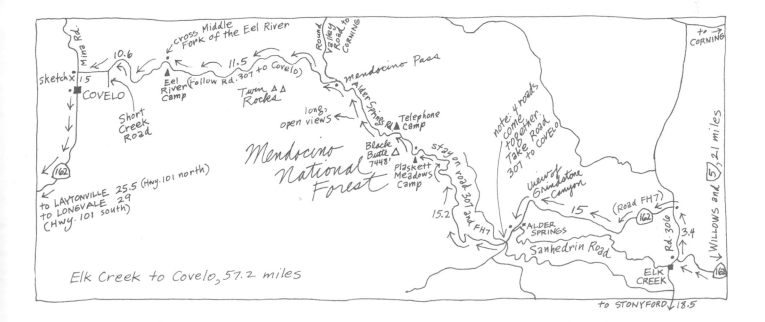

Elk Creek to Covelo, 57.2 miles

48

The road to Blocksburg

North of Garberville, in the Avenue of the Giants, I draw an almost 8-foot-wide redwood stump. Over the years countless initials have been carved in the wood. One carving is somewhat more profound than the others. It states "Thou art God."

Leaving the great redwoods, I travel inland through hilly forest and meadow. Big views of mountain scenery appear, sometimes on both sides of the road as I drive higher. They are awe-inspiring. I bypass Fort Seward, a military post in 1861.

Redwoods, Humboldt County

At Blocksburg I get permission to sketch the town's oldest barn and march across a field of thistles and manure piles to sit in the shade of an old fruit tree. At the time the barn was built the town had seven bars and two barbershops. It was a tanbark-collecting center from which the bark was hauled to a faraway tannery in Willits. Sheep raising was big also and there was some manganese ore mining. The old Mail Ridge Stage Route north from San Francisco passed through here when Mr. Blocksburgher, the town's namesake, had been a storekeeper and wool merchant.

From Bridgeville—also a stop on the old Mail Ridge Stage Route—I climb up a long, steep gravel road. The climb is worth it for I am now richly rewarded with vast mountain views. Metal barn roofs glisten in the distance. I pass the charming community of Freshwater on my journey to Eureka.

Blocksburg barn,
Humboldt County

50

51

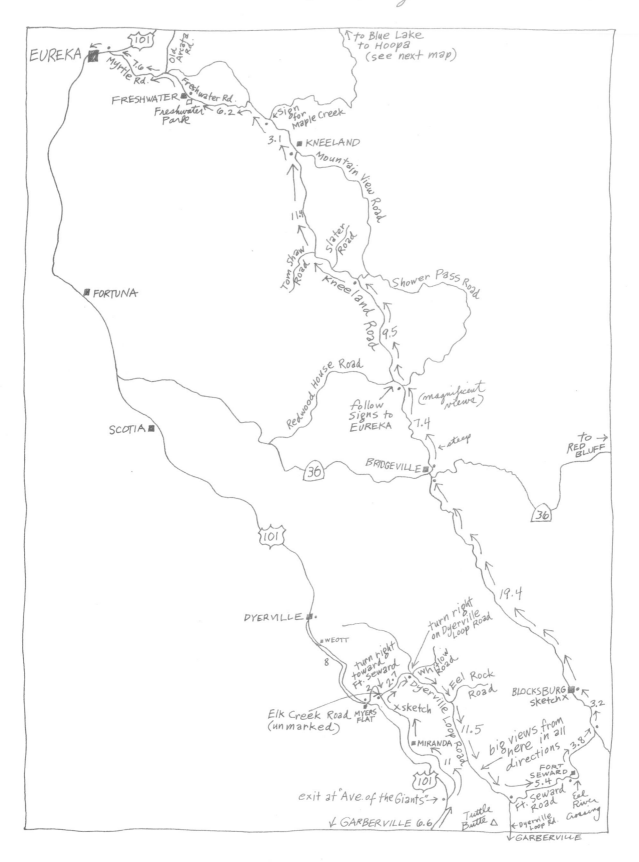

The road to Hoopa Valley and to Lady Bird Johnson Grove

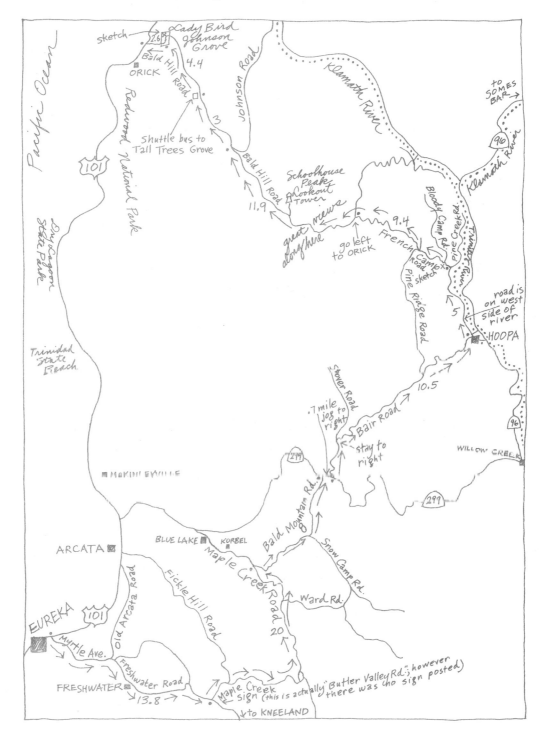

54

Hoopa Valley, Humboldt County   55

The road to Hoopa Valley (map, page 53)

Butler Valley Road east of Eureka meanders north. A winding mountain road then proceeds across the Mad River and picturesque Maple Creek. Near Lord Ellis Summit, forest foliage joins overhead to become a tunnel of green. Firs, cedars, tanbark, oak, and madrone line Bair Road to Hoopa Valley. Leaving Hoopa, I sketch a view with the Klamath River glinting in the sun, winding its way through the green valley, fine mountain scenery all around. A madrone tree offers shade and drops stiff, dry leaves about me with each slight breeze.

Hoopa Valley to Lady Bird Johnson Grove (map, page 53)

The long pull uphill from Hoopa Valley finally emerges on top of the world (or so it seems!). The views exhilarate and lift the spirit. I travel through high pastureland and descend near the coast to Lady Bird Johnson Grove. There I draw a so-called Goose Pen Tree (redwood), which pioneers had, on occasion, used to confine small livestock and fowl. Oxalis, sword fern, salal, and evergreen huckleberry grow at its redwood base. Scarred by ancient fires, the tree itself remains alive and well, a giant in this truly magnificent stand of redwoods. Experiencing this place is enriching and inspiring.

Goose Pen redwood, Humboldt County

The Salmon Alps, Siskiyou County

Back road along the Salmon River to Scott Valley

From Somes Bar and Highway 96 and from Forks of Salmon to Cecilville, a narrow, paved, winding, sometimes one-way road clings to the rocky ledge high above the roaring Salmon River. A sign early on had warned motorists that slow travel and honking of the horn on blind curves might be necessary.

Views of the Salmon Alps appear as I approach Cecilville. From Cecilville the road becomes straighter and smoother (and thereby less interesting). At the Salmon Summit and the Pacific Crest Trailhead heliport I sketch 7,790-foot Eagle Peak and include Billy's Peak and Battle Mountain. They are all lined up in splendid array from this scenic viewpoint.

I descend from here to Callahan at the foot of Scott Valley.

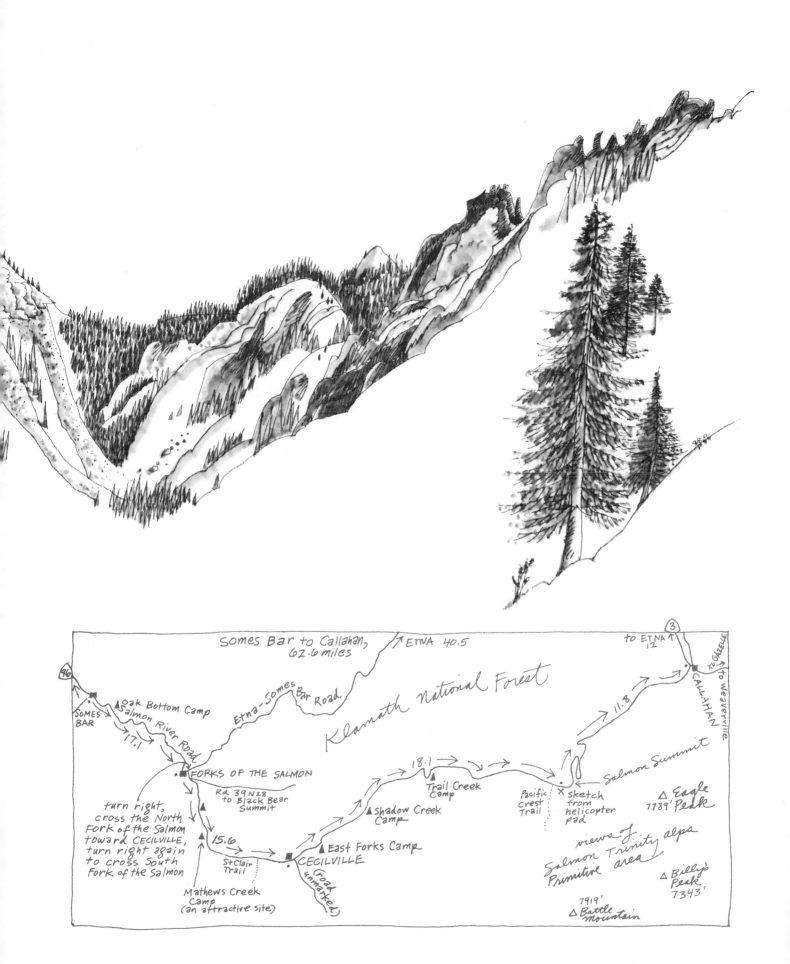

Somes Bar to Callahan, 62.6 miles → ETNA 40.5

to ETNA 12 3

to GAZELLE
to Weaverville
CALLAHAN

96

Klamath National Forest

SOMES BAR
Oak Bottom Camp
Salmon River Road
Etna-Somes Bar Road
17.1

11.8

Salmon Summit

FORKS OF THE SALMON

Rd 39N28 to Black Bear Summit

18.1 →

Trail Creek Camp

Pacific Crest Trail

X sketch from helicopter pad

△ Eagle 7789' Peak

turn right, cross the North Fork of the Salmon toward CECILVILLE, turn right again to cross South Fork of the Salmon

▲ Shadow Creek Camp

▲ East Forks Camp

views of Salmon Trinity Alps Primitive area

StClair Trail

CECILVILLE (road unmarked)

△ Billy's Peak 7343'

15.6 →

Mathews Creek Camp (an attractive site)

7919' △ Battle Mountain

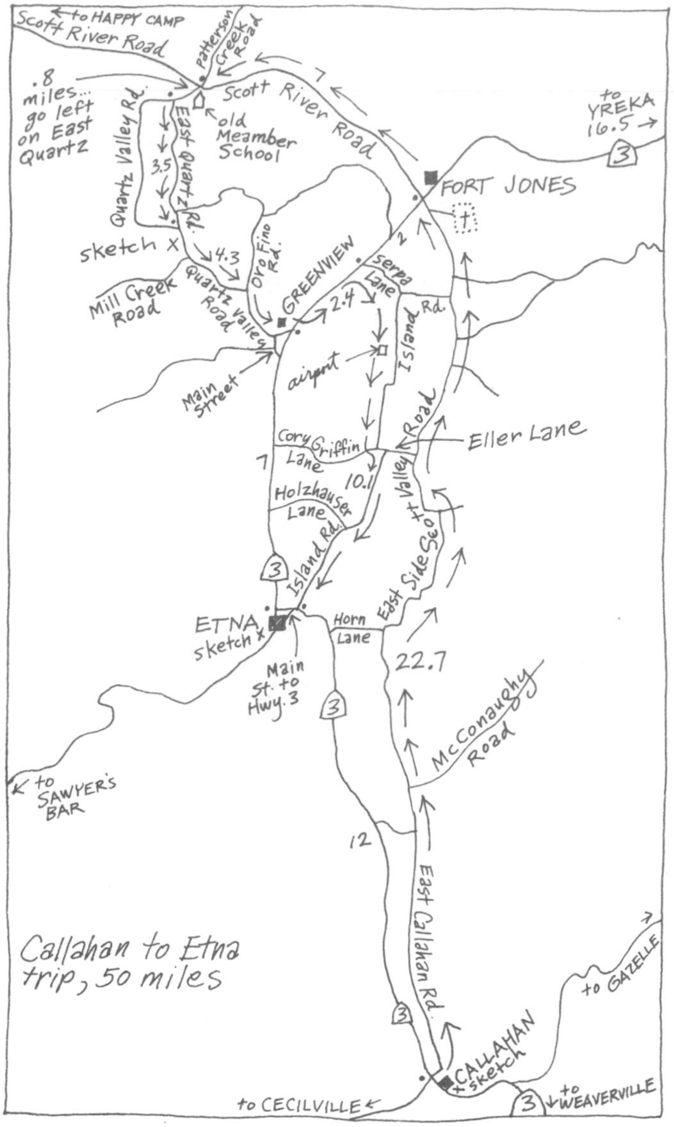

to HAPPY CAMP
Scott River Road
Patterson Creek Road
.8 miles... go left on East Quartz
Quartz Valley Rd.
East Quartz Rd.
old Meamber School
Scott River Road
7
to YREKA 16.5
3
FORT JONES
3.5
sketch X
4.3
Oro Fino Rd.
Mill Creek Road
Quartz Valley Road
GREENVIEW
2
Serpa Lane
2.4
Island Rd.
airport
Main Street
Cory Griffin Lane
Eller Lane
7
10.1
Holzhauser Lane
Island Rd.
East Side Scott Valley Road
3
ETNA
sketch X
Horn Lane
Main St. to Hwy. 3
22.7
3
McConaughy Road
to SAWYER'S BAR
12
East Callahan Rd.
Callahan to Etna trip, 50 miles
to GAZELLE
3
CALLAHAN
sketch
to CECILVILLE
3
to WEAVERVILLE

a trip through Scott Valley

The valley was named for John Scott, who had led a group of miners into the area in 1850. He discovered gold, and Scott Valley became a rich mining region. Today the valley is green with agricultural crops. Sprinklers sprinkle and black angus cows browse in the field.

In Quartz Valley, where gold camps once flourished, I sketch a neat, white schoolhouse and its monumental stone marker.

At Etna, originally known as Rough and Ready Mills, I draw the library building with its massive flagpole. As you approach the town, you can see the pole towering over all the other structures. I asked at the post office, city hall, and finally, a corner delicatessan to find out the height of the pole. The gentleman who told me it was 136½ feet (two feet shorter than the one at neighboring Fort Jones) wondered whether I wanted to climb it. I said no, but I'd enjoy seeing someone else do it!

White Schoolhouse, Siskiyou County

Etna's flagpole,
Siskiyou County

ETNA FREE LIBRARY and READING ROOM

Sign at Callahan, Siskiyou County

Back road from Scott Valley.

The Farrington Blacksmith Shop, the General Store, and the Ranch Hotel still stand at Callahan. I draw the old sign over the post office entrance next to the General Store and chat with the owner whose great-grandfather had built these historic edifices. In the 1860s this locality was a stage stop along the principal wagon road north to Oregon.

The road going east from Callahan rises gently to almost 5,000 feet through pine and cedar forest, then suddenly drops toward Interstate 5 near Gazelle.

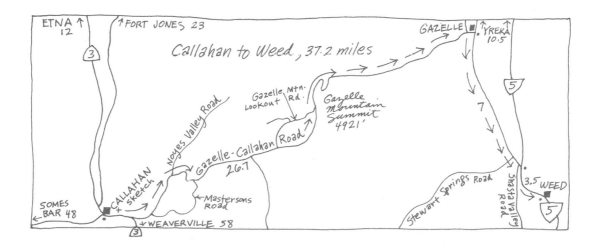

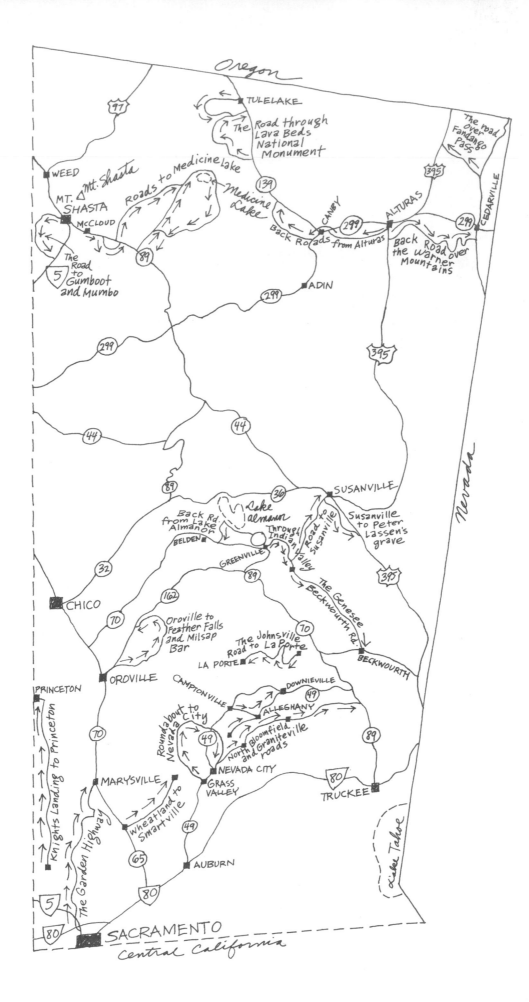

Oregon

TULELAKE

The Road through Lava Beds National Monument

97

The road over Fandango Pass

WEED
Mt. Shasta

Roads to Medicine Lake

MT. SHASTA

McCLOUD

139

Medicine Lake

CANBY

299

ALTURAS

395

CEDARVILLE

299

The Road to Gumboot and Mumbo

5

89

Back Roads from Alturas

Back Road over the Warner Mountains

299

ADIN

299

299

44

395

44

89

SUSANVILLE

36

Lake Almanor

Back Rd. from Lake Almanor

Susanville to Peter Lassen's grave

Through Indian Valley

Road to Susanville

BELDEN

32

GREENVILLE

89

395

CHICO

162

The Genesee

Beckwourth Rd.

70

70

Oroville to Feather Falls and Milsap Bar

The Johnsville Road to La Porte

LA PORTE

BECKWOURTH

OROVILLE

CAMPTONVILLE

DOWNIEVILLE

49

PRINCETON

Roundabout to Nevada City

ALLEGHANY

49

North Bloomfield and Graniteville roads

89

70

49

NEVADA CITY

80

MARYSVILLE

GRASS VALLEY

TRUCKEE

Knights Landing to Princeton

Wheatland to Smartville

49

Lake Tahoe

The Garden Highway

65

AUBURN

5

80

80

80

SACRAMENTO

Central California

64

Northeastern California

It is heartening to think that however loud the main arteries of traffic may become, there are back roads existing in quietude and natural beauty. I leave the insistent, fretful clamor of the freeway and travel the lonely back roads. Their untainted atmosphere and the closeness of trees and roadside flowers are of infinite attraction to me. It wouldn't be practical to pave or straighten these roads. They serve no profitable purpose, and for that I am thankful.

Monkey flower, Placer County

Castle Crags, Siskiyou County

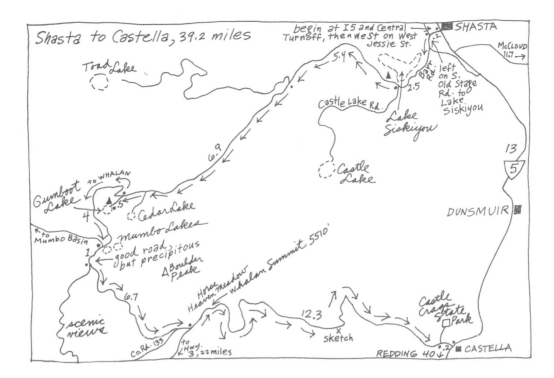

Shasta to Castella, 39.2 miles

begin at I5 and Central Turnoff, then West on West Jessie St.

SHASTA

McCLOUD 11.7 →

Toad Lake

5.4

left on S. Old Stage Rd. to Lake Siskiyou

2.5

Castle Lake Rd.

Lake Siskiyou

6.9

13

5

Castle Lake

to WHALAN

Gumboot Lake

4

Cedar Lake

Mumbo Lakes

DUNSMUIR

to Mumbo Basin

1

good road but precipitous

△ Boulder Peak

Horse Heaven Meadow   Whalan Summit 5510'

6.7

12.3

scenic views

Co.Rd. 133

to ↓ Hwy. 3, 22 miles

X sketch

Castle Crags State Park

CASTELLA

REDDING 40 ↓

The road to Gumboot and Mumbo

I pass tranquil Lake Siskiyou and ascend the rugged, rocky canyon. A rushing stream tumbles and splashes downward on my left. Gumboot Lake, cradled in granite in this high mountain wilderness, deeply reflects the blue of the sky. There are views near Mumbo Lake of far distant mountain ranges of northern California, including the high Trinity Alps. Finally I see the impressive Castle Crags and stop to draw its soft gray-colored prominence in the early morning light. It has been a fine trip for the beauty of mountain places, long views, and impressive high country forests.

Roads to Medicine Lake

The trip to Medicine Lake begins with stops to view McCloud River Falls. Upper and Lower Falls are easy enough to find; Middle Falls, however, is not marked. The roar can be heard from the roadway, so I follow the sound. There is a sheer cliff to be wary of and therefore this is no place for small children. All three falls are well worth viewing as they churn over rock ledges with a resounding roar. But Middle and Upper Falls are the most dramatic.

There are three routes from the McCloud area to Medicine Lake. Route 13, the road I follow, is dusty but affords closer views of Mount Shasta.

I see Paint Pot Crater, just visible from the road at one point, then Pumice Mountain. On Medicine Lake Road I pass at the very foot of Little Glass Mountain where great black chunks of obsidian glisten in the sunshine.

Back road musician,
Lower Falls, Siskiyou County

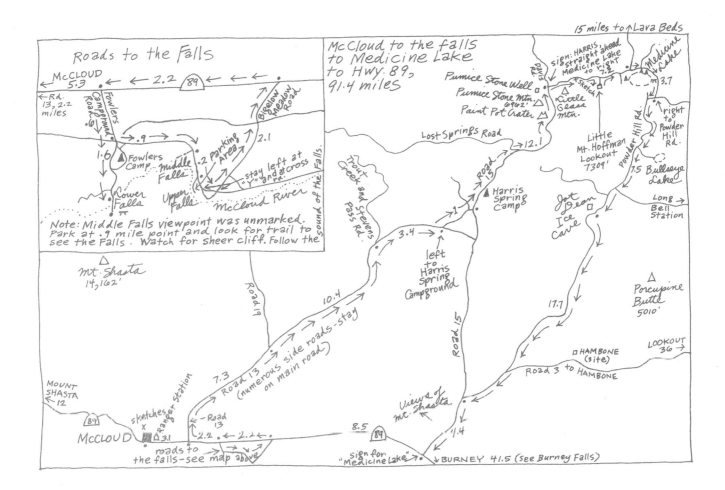

Roads to the Falls

McCLOUD 5.3 ← ← 2.2 ← (89) ← ← ← ← •

Rd. 13, 2.2 miles

Fowlers Campground Road

Bigelow Meadow Road

→ .9 → → ↑ 2.1

1.6 ↑ Fowlers Camp ▲ middle Falls ← .2 parking Area →

stay left at "Y" and cross rd.

Lower Falls ⊓ Upper Falls McCloud River

sound of the Falls

Note: Middle Falls viewpoint was unmarked. Park at .9 mile point and look for trail to see the Falls. Watch for sheer cliff. Follow the

Mt. Shasta 14,162'

Road 19

Trout and Stevens Creek Pass Rd.

10.4 →

7.3 → Road 13 (numerous side roads - stay on main road)

MOUNT SHASTA ← 12

sketches or station X

(89) McCLOUD ▦ △ 3.1

Ranger station

Road 13 2.2 → • ← 2.2 ← •

roads to the falls - see map above

8.5 (89)

sign for "Medicine Lake" →

↓ BURNEY 41.5 (see Burney Falls)

McCloud to the falls to Medicine Lake to Hwy. 89, 91.4 miles

Pumice Stone Well Pumice Stone Mtn. 6962' Paint Pot Crater

Lost Springs Road → 12.1

sign: HARRIS straight ahead Medicine Lake to right 7.2

Davis Rd.

Medicine Lake

sketch

Little Glass mtn.

m 3.7

right to Powder Hill Rd.

Powder Hill Rd.

Little Mt. Hoffman Lookout 7309'

7.5 Bullseye Lake

Long Bell Station

Road 13

Harris Spring Camp ▲

← 1

3.4 → •

left to Harris Spring Campground

Jot Dean Ice Cave

Road 15

17.7 ↓

△ Porcupine Butte 5010'

☐ HAMBONE (site)

Road 3 to HAMBONE

LOOKOUT 36

Views of Mt. Shasta •

↓ 1.4

I stop to sketch a particularly dramatic view of Mount Shasta, the helter-skelter profile of Little Glass Mountain in the middle distance. At Little Mount Hoffman lookout a 360-degree view of the world is presented below. The less-than-a-mile drive to the lookout, though precipitous, should be done.

The view of the entire Little Glass Mountain lava flow is particularly interesting from this point.

Medicine Lake proves a lovely, protected, bright blue body of water, and there's a good view of it from the picnic grounds. You have the option of either going further to see Lava Beds National Monument or returning toward McCloud. Jot Dean Ice Cave is on the way to McCloud. It has its own mystic sense of beauty with subtle colorings and dripping sound effects.

Mount Shasta, Siskiyou County

In McCloud I explore the streets of this quaint company town. I travel out East Columbero, go north on Shasta and east on Mill Street.

Past the big mill I follow Firenze Street and North Street back to the mill. Following West Columbero, I take Hennessy Way to Tucci, Walnut, and Oak. I draw the Bradshaw House, former lumber executive residence near Lawndale Court off Main, and the log church. It occurs to me that the chocolate brown church with its whipped cream colored seams actually looks quite appetizing.

The Bradshaw House, McCloud, Siskiyou County

St. Joseph's, the chocolate brown church,
McCloud, Siskiyou County

75

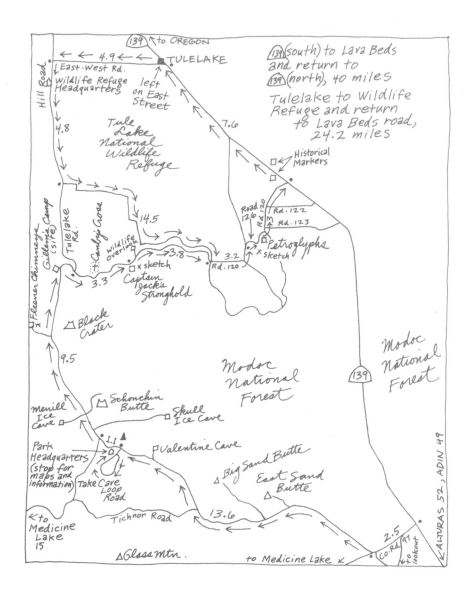

The road through Lava Beds National Monument

There are some 14 or 15 caves to explore near park headquarters. Mushpot Cave is well lit, but flashlights are a necessity for the others. They have colorful names which invite exploration, like Golden Dome, Hopkins Chocolate, and Hercules Leg.

I sketch at Captain Jack's Stronghold, where the Modoc tribe made the U.S. Army pay dearly for victory over the intransigent Indians. As I walk the path through the stronghold I realize how 60 rugged Indians could hold back an army of 600 for five months.

Captain Jack's Stronghold,
Siskiyou and Modoc Counties   77

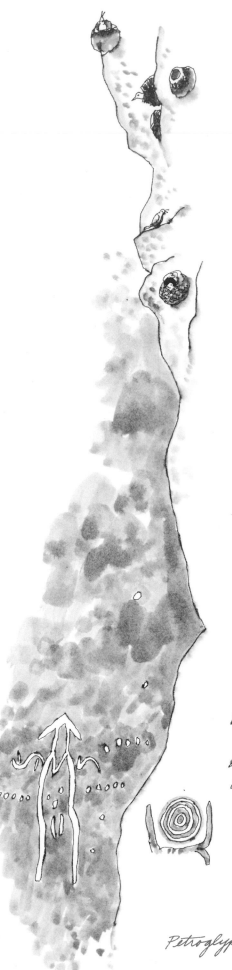

If it's not too late in the day and you're not in a rush to go on, you could double back to the Tulelake Road (see map) and take the Wildlife Tour Route back to Lava Beds Monument. Otherwise, it might be best to stay overnight in Tulelake and leave the Wildlife Tour for the next day, which is what I decide to do.

At the Petroglyphs I sketch ancient markings, enjoying their simple designs. I watch swallows flying around their mud nests.

On the Wildlife Tour I see ducks of all sorts, herons, white pelicans, Canadian geese, varieties of seabirds, thousands of shiny blue dragonflies, locusts, bees, and a lively assortment of unnamed creatures.

Petroglyphs, Lava Beds National Monument, Modoc County

Back road over the Warner Mountains

I leave Alturas and stop at scenic Dorris Reservoir. The surface of the reservoir is placid, the morning sun glinting off the water. A flight of honking geese make a "V" formation overhead. Grazing horses on a nearby shore look like cutouts on the horizon.

The Warner Mountains in the distance, snow still lingering on Squaw Peak, beckon me. The road goes through juniper and pine forest, crosses several streams, and gently ascends into the Warners.

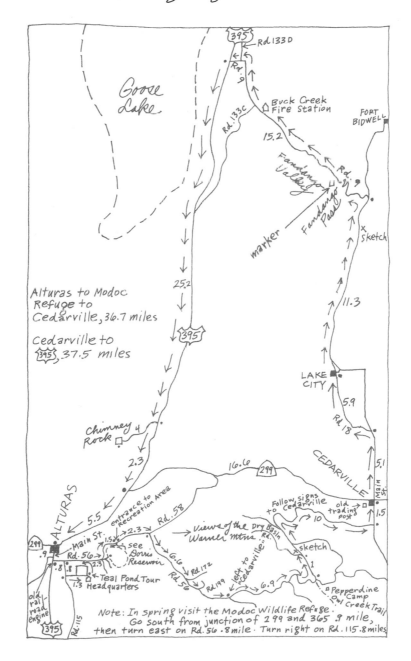

Goose Lake

Alturas to Modoc Refuge to Cedarville, 36.7 miles

Cedarville to 395, 37.5 miles

Rd. 133 D

Rd. 9

Buck Creek Fire Station

FORT BIDWELL

15.2

Fandango Valley

Rd. 9

marker

Fandango Pass

× sketch

11.3

LAKE CITY

5.9

Rd. 18

25.2

395

Chimney Rock

2.3

16.6

299

CEDARVILLE

5.1

Main St.

ALTURAS

5.5

entrance to Recreation Area

Rd. 58

Views of the Dry Basin Warner Mtns

Follow signs to Cedarville

old trading post

1.5

10

299

.9

Rd. 56

1.5

2.3

see Dorris Reservoir

6.6

Rd. 56

Rd. 172

Rd. 199

left to Cedarville

6.9

sketch

1

.8

.8

2.3

Teal Pond Tour Headquarters

1.3

Pepperdine Camp Owl Creek Trail

old railroad engine

395

Rd. 115

Note: In spring visit the Modoc Wildlife Refuge. Go south from junction of 299 and 365 .9 mile, then turn east on Rd. 56 .8 mile. Turn right on Rd. 115 .8 miles

At the summit I draw a twisted and all but downed juniper. It expresses well the ferocity of winter storms at this altitude. Grasshoppers make clicking noises, an unseen bird sings, a cool light breeze whooshes through the pines, flies buzz, and range cattle come to stare at me.

From this point the road levels off, then descends toward Cedarville in Surprise Valley. Wagon trains came through here in the 1860s, and James Townsend built a trading post in 1865. He was killed by Indians in 1866. William Cressler and John Bonner bought the Townsend building in 1867 and turned it into a combination trading post and store. What is left of it can still be seen in the town park on Center Street between Highway 299 and Bonner Street.

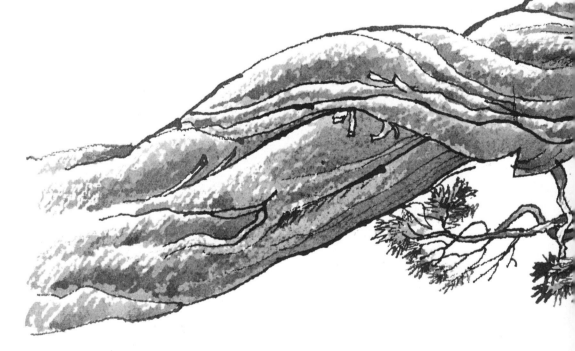

Twisted juniper,
Warner Mountains, Modoc County

The road over Fandango Pass *(see map, page 79)*

I travel from Cedarville to the hamlet of Lake City, enjoying sweeping views of Surprise Valley and Upper Lake. Early pioneers were surprised to find a green valley after leaving the barren landscape of Nevada; thereby the name, Surprise Valley. I sketch the inventive antelope and deer horn arrangement at the Hanks Ranch and talk to a charming 88-year-old ranch woman who looks every bit the pioneer in big, floppy hat and one-piece dress. Her gnarled hands point to some cows and calves moving past. She is worried about the whereabouts of a particular calf.

HANKS RANCH

Back road ranch sign, Modoc County

The approach to Fandango is steep. The Peter
Lassen and Applegate trails come together here, then
part again on the other side of the Warners.
Lassen goes south, Applegate north.   A massacre took
place along this trail sometime between 1846 and 1850.
It is said that Indians attacked while pioneers were
dancing the fandango. The fandangoists were completely
wiped out.   Today I enjoy the sweeping view across
Fandango Valley; cows grazing on the opposite side
look like slowly moving specks.

Back Roads from Alturas

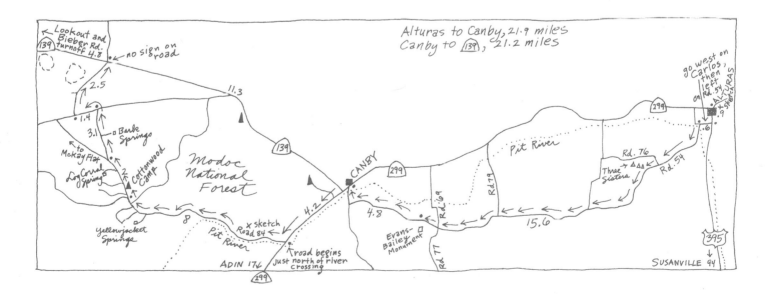

Alturas to Canby, 21.9 miles
Canby to 139, 21.2 miles

The Court House, Alturas, Modoc County

Back roads of Alturas — (map, page 83)

Before leaving Alturas, I admire the solidly elegant bulk of the Modoc County Court House. To sketch it I gain permission to sit on the lawn surrounding the chalk white golden-domed building. 1914 is the date on its facade, and F. J. DeLongchamps was the architect. Niles Hotel is another notable building in Alturas. When you visit the Chamber of Commerce you are in the original County Recorder Office of Modoc County. To the rear is the old jail. I travel the Centerville Road west and enjoy broad views of agricultural land and juniper forest. Yellow daisies line the roadway at times, pretty faces turned to the morning sun.

On a hill to the south a white marker commemorates the death of S.D. Evans and Joe Bailey, killed by Indians in July 1861 while driving 900 head of beef cattle to the mines in Virginia City, Nevada.

NAVY ITS NOT JUST A JOB ITS AN ADVENTURE

GO AIR FORCE

USAF REC OFFICE

Going west I reach Canby, named for
the U.S. General of the Modoc War, and
turn left to locate County Road 84 and
the Pit River. I enjoy the scenery along
the lazily flowing stream and pause to
draw one of the views. Cows scratching their
backs on low juniper branches stop to moo.
Only two cowboys in pickup trucks pass
in one and a half hours. The road has
the essence of an old covered wagon trail.
(map, page 83)

The Pit River, Modoc County

Back road from Lake Almanor

    The road hugs the shore of Butt Valley Reservoir. It is a pretty body of water despite the eye-jarring power-line structures. I cross the dam spillway and proceed down toward the rushing Feather River. What a colossal canyon! I descend steep slopes with views of forested mountainsides and clouds feathering out along mountain tops. At Caribou, an attractive PG&E Company village, there is a sign, "Fishermen Welcome." I picnic nearby with a view of the Forebay and the impressive cliffs opposite. I continue along the road, stopping to watch a gold-sluicing operation in the river. The road ends at Highway 70 near Belden town and the Eby Stamp Mill roadside rest.

Road block,
Plumas County

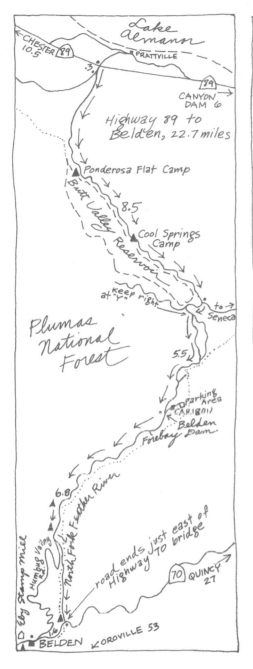

Lake Almanor

CHESTER 10.5 [89]

PRATTVILLE

.3

[89] CANYON DAM 6

Highway 89 to
Belden, 22.7 miles

▲ Ponderosa Flat Camp

8.5

Butt Valley Reservoir

▲ Cool Springs Camp

at Y, keep right

to Seneca

5.5

Plumas National Forest

□ Parking Area
▲ CARIBOU
Belden Forebay Dam

6.8

North Fork Feather River

Eby Stamp Mill
Humbug Valley Rd.

road ends just east of
Highway 70 bridge

[70] QUINCY 27

.16

□ ▲ BELDEN   ← OROVILLE 53

Indian Valley map

[89]

← Pecks Valley Rd.

Williams Valley Rd.

Main St.

Setzer Rd.

Beckwourth-Greenville Road

□ Indian Mission

× sketch   → 18

Greenville to
Taylorsville
21.7 miles

[89] GREENVILLE

3

Round Valley Road

▲ Round Valley Reservoir

Long Valley Road

Indian Valley

4

Stampfli Lane 3

2 ■ CRESCENT MILLS

Arlington Road [A22] 5

[89]

← QUINCY 17

SUSANVILLE →

Diamond Mt. Rd.

1.6

.7

North Arm
East Side Rd.

.3

1.1

TAYLORSVILLE
sketch × [i] ∏

to Beckwourth ↓

Back road through Indian Valley

I travel from Greenville, long a center of quartz mining activity. It has a distinctive California mining and lumber town look about it. The town is located at one end of broad and beautiful Indian Valley. In winter there are views of surrounding snow-capped peaks. I stop to sketch old Wheelock Shingle Mill with Mount Hough and Grizzly Peak in the background.

The old Wheelock Shingle Mill,
Indian Valley, Plumas County

91

At Taylorsville I search the
pioneer cemetery for the monument
marking the grave of the town's namesake, Jobe
Taylor, who settled here in 1852. (I find it.)
This is a village of quaint rural charm with
old houses along shady streets, a white
steepled church, and many barns.

Taylorsville Community Church, 1875

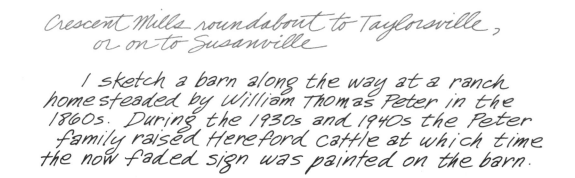

Crescent Mills roundabout to Taylorsville,
or on to Susanville

   I sketch a barn along the way at a ranch
homesteaded by William Thomas Peter in the
1860s. During the 1930s and 1940s the Peter
family raised Hereford cattle at which time
the now faded sign was painted on the barn.

Crescent Mills to Susanville, 34.8 miles

HWY 44 89
44
6
SUSANVILLE
4.5
Gold Run Rd.
36
4
to ALTURAS 94
395
Rd. to Moonlight V.
Rd. to Fleming Sheep Camp
Peter Lassen grave
9
395
Lake Almanor 38
36
Rd. to Westwood
15.4
Rd. to Morton Creek
road quality on the primitive side
JANESVILLE
Road to Shake Cabin
Road to Antelope Lake
Road to Moonlight Valley
3 roads come together, take road on left to Susanville
Engle Mine ruins
5.4
Antelope Lake
CANYON DAM 9
89
sketch X
5
Diamond Mtn Road
North Arm East Side Rd.
GREENVILLE
4 89
Stampfli Lane
X sketch
6.2
Note: This is an alternate drive back to Taylorsville if you elect not to drive the primitive road to Susanville.
CRESCENT MILLS
4.5
TAYLORSVILLE
sometimes
QUINCY 23
BECKWOURTH

Hereford Ranch barn, near Taylorsville, Plumas County

The North Arm of Indian Valley is a grand, green expanse bounded by forested mountains.

I draw the valley in the silent, sunny morning. Ants crawl up my legs, bees hum, and the work of woodpeckers echoes across the valley.

You can return to Indian Valley via North Arm East Side Road at the valley's end.

I choose to go over the mountains to Susanville. The road becomes primitive in places; eventually the pine forest thins out, and I descend to the pleasant farming country around Susanville.

The North Arm of Indian Valley, Plumas County

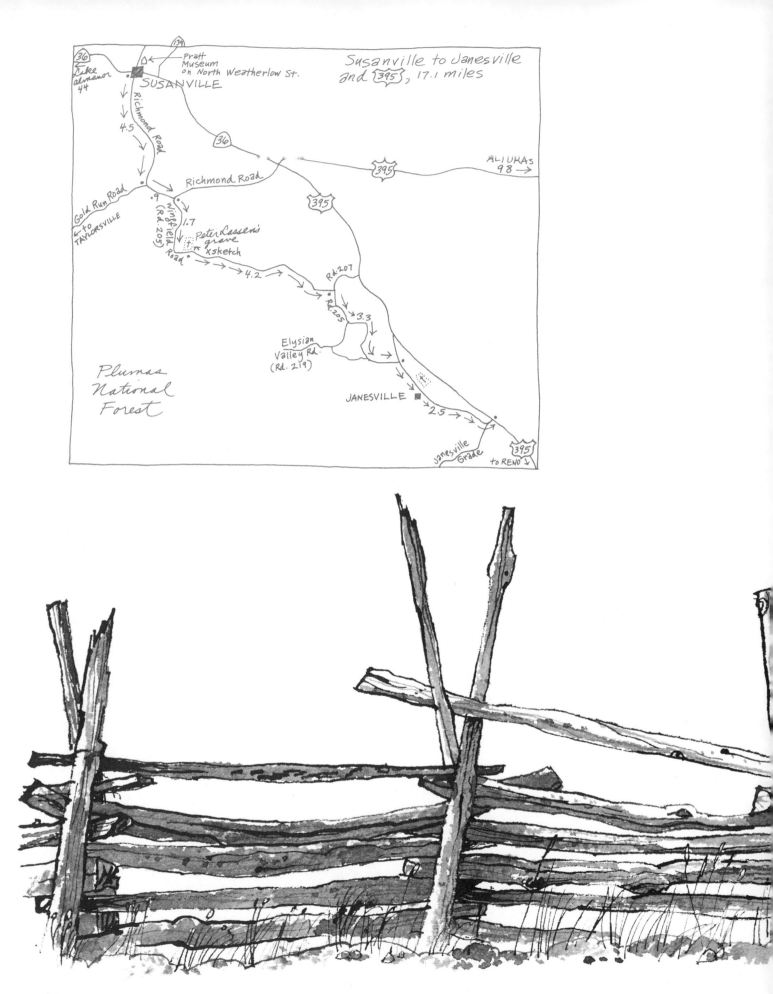

Susanville to Janesville and (395), 17.1 miles

(36) Lake almanor 44

(139)

△ → Pratt Museum on North Weatherlow St.

SUSANVILLE

Richmond Road

4.5

(36)

ALTURAS 98 →

(395)

Richmond Road

Gold Run Road to TAYLORSVILLE

.9

Wingfield (Rd. 205)

1.7

Peter Lassen's grave x sketch

(395)

Peter Lassen's grave Road

4.2

Rd. 207

Rd. 205

3.3

Elysian Valley Rd. (Rd. 219)

JANESVILLE

2.5

Plumas National Forest

Janesville Grade

to RENO ↓

(395)

Susanville to Peter Lassen's grave and Janesville

Isaac Roop was the first white settler in Honey Lake Valley. Susanville, in fact, was named for his first daughter. The Roop log cabin still stands in the city park on Weatherlow Street as does the William Pratt Memorial Museum.

I travel from here to Peter Lassen's grave. Lassen came here from Denmark when he was 29, lived in Indian Valley for awhile and then settled in this area in 1855. Unfortunately, it may not have been a good choice since he was killed here by Indians on April 26, 1859, at age 66.

I sketch a decorative rail fence, to the harmonies of mooing cows, on my way to the interesting community of Janesville. A rancher, mending fences, stops long enough to shake his head and comment on my drawing: "Well, that's another way to earn a living, I guess."

Split rail fence near Susanville, Lassen County

The Genesee-Beckwourth Road

In Genesee Valley I find idyllic farm scenery with grazing cows and sheep, old barns, and old farms. There is still a good collection of buildings marking the former hamlet of Genesee. I continue on Beckwourth Road, crossing a creek full of big granite boulders at Drum Bridge. The landscape changes dramatically farther along when great lava outcroppings appear. The forest becomes sparse, and gray-green sagebrush patterns the landscape. I come across horses in the road! Then deer and fawns leap across the way.

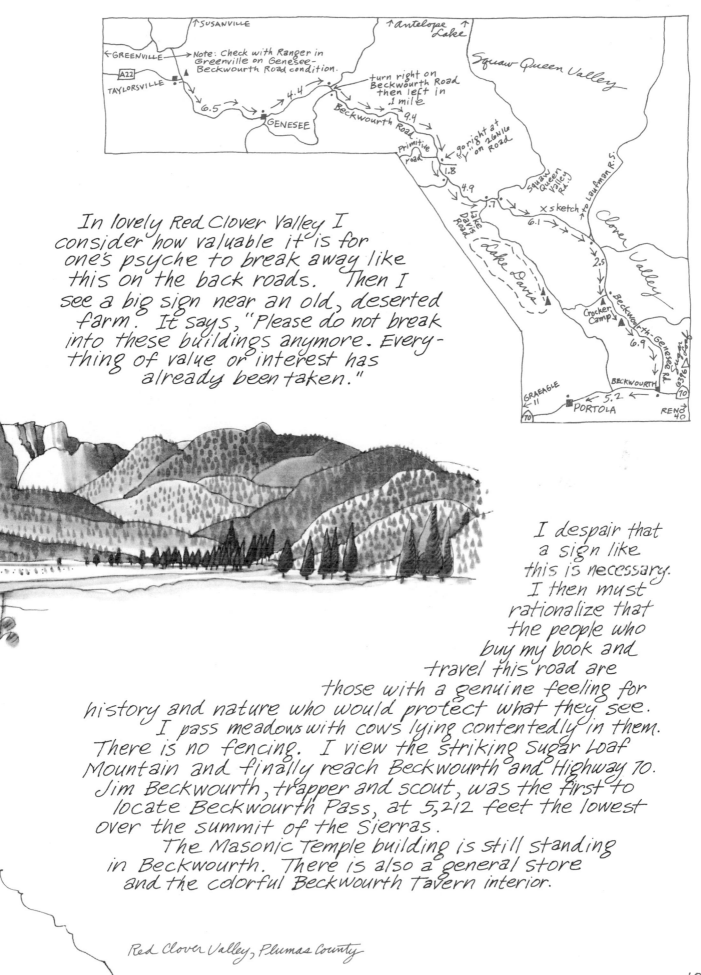

In the map:

↑SUSANVILLE

←GREENVILLE → Note: Check with Ranger in Greenville on Genesee-Beckwourth Road condition.

A22

TAYLORSVILLE

6.5

GENESEE

4.4

↑antelope Lake ↑

turn right on Beckwourth Road then left in .1 mile

Beckwourth Road

9.4

Squaw Queen Valley

Primitive road

go right at "Y" on 2.6 mile Road

1.8

4.9

.7

Squaw Queen Valley Rd.

X sketch to Lautman R.S.

sketch to Lautman R.S.

6.1

Clover Valley

2.5

Lake Davis Road

Lake Davis

Crocker Camp

Beckwourth-Genesee Rd.

6.9

Sugar Loaf

9396 ↑ Sugar Loaf

BECKWOURTH

70

GRAEAGLE ←11

PORTOLA

70

← 5.2 ←

RENO 40

In lovely Red Clover Valley I consider how valuable it is for one's psyche to break away like this on the back roads. Then I see a big sign near an old, deserted farm. It says, "Please do not break into these buildings anymore. Everything of value or interest has already been taken."

I despair that a sign like this is necessary. I then must rationalize that the people who buy my book and travel this road are those with a genuine feeling for history and nature who would protect what they see. I pass meadows with cows lying contentedly in them. There is no fencing. I view the striking Sugar Loaf Mountain and finally reach Beckwourth and Highway 70. Jim Beckwourth, trapper and scout, was the first to locate Beckwourth Pass, at 5,212 feet the lowest over the summit of the Sierras.

The Masonic Temple building is still standing in Beckwourth. There is also a general store and the colorful Beckwourth Tavern interior.

Red Clover Valley, Plumas County

101

102

Johnsville, Plumas County

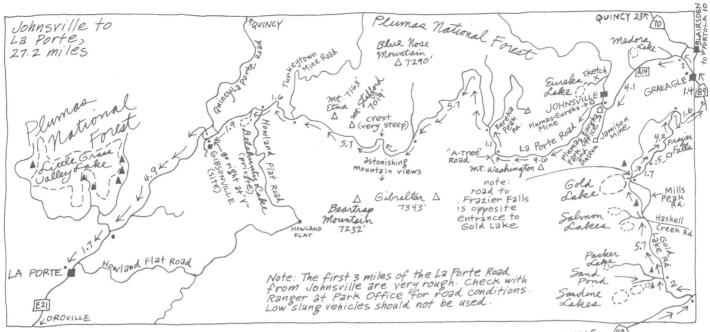

Johnsville to
La Porte,
27.2 miles

QUINCY 23

QUINCY

Plumas National Forest

Blue Nose
Mountain
△ 7290'

Medora
Lake

BLAIRSDEN 10
to PORTOLA 10

70

A14

Eureka
Lake

sketch
X

4.1

GRAEAGLE

1.4

89

Plumas
National
Forest

Turkeytown Mine Road

Quincy-La Porte Road

Mt. 7163
Etna △

Mt. Stafford
7019'

crest
(very steep)

5.7

Eureka
Peak

JOHNSVILLE

Plumas-Eureka
Mine

Plumas-Eureka
Park Office

La Porte Road

Jamison
Mine

4.2

Frazier
Falls

1.6

Howland Flat Road

Bechdolly Creek (private)

1.6

1.9

"8 miles at 'Y'"

GIBSONVILLE
(site)

5.7

5.7

astonishing
mountain views

1.1

"A-Tree"
Road

4.6

Mt. Washington △

.5

1.7

4.9

Little Grass
Valley Lake

Beartrap
Mountain
7232'

△ Gibralter △
7343'

note:
road to
Frazier Falls
is opposite
entrance to
Gold Lake

Gold
Lake

Mills
Peak
Rd.

Salmon
Lakes

Haskell
Creek Rd.

1.7

HOWLAND
FLAT

LA PORTE

Howland Flat Road

Note: The first 3 miles of the La Porte Road
from Johnsville are very rough. Check with
Ranger at Park Office for road conditions.
Low slung vehicles should not be used.

Packer
Lake

Sand
Pond

Sardine
Lakes

5.7

2

E21

OROVILLE

DOWNIEVILLE
about 17 miles

49

The Johnsville Road to La Porte

I travel Gold Lake Road to the fabled lake whose shoreline
was supposedly covered with chunks of gold. This was according
to a J.R. Stoddard, who had stumbled across such a lake,
he said, somewhere between Downieville and Sierra Valley
in 1849. It was never found, yet the name Gold Lake was
given to this lovely body of water.

I take the road opposite the lake to Frazier Falls.
A ½-mile hike takes me to a good view of the 248-foot cascade
of water. Graeagle is close by and so are the old mining town
of Johnsville and Plumas-Eureka State Park.

I stop to draw Johnsville and Mount Washington from
the road to Eureka Lake. At the park museum are Snowshoe
Thompson's 25-pound skis, which he used to carry the mail
across the Sierras in wintertime. He did this for five
years beginning in 1856, skiing from Placerville to Carson
Valley, Nevada, and back. After a visit to the museum, I
inspect portions of the nearby Plumas-Eureka mine, where
millions of dollars in gold were produced.

"The first three miles are the bumpiest," I am told by
the ranger at the State Park, as we discuss the road to La
Porte. He's right. I drive at much less than ten miles per hour.

I listen to a classical music station beaming Beethoven's
Emperor concerto from Reno, Nevada. My spirit is filled with
the beauty of it all. It should never be made an
easier trip. I finally reach the crest of this high
Sierra journey——a bit steep but maneuverable——and later
pass the site of Gibsonville town on the road to La Porte.

103

Oroville to Feather Falls and Milsap Bar
(map, page 106)

The town of Feather Falls is attractively unified in design with each building painted barn red with white trim. Proceeding toward Milsap Bar along a particularly dusty stretch of road, a man astride a small motorcycle approaches. He slows and I slow to minimize dust. He stops. I stop. We chat in the middle of the road. He is the friendly owner of the Cascade Saloon, and I am intrigued enough by his description of the place to locate and draw it.

It is 19 miles to a telephone from here and there is no electricity. The beer is quite cold, however, for there is plenty of bottled gas to keep the power going. I watch bumblebees in the flower garden, have a beer, and sit in the shade of a colossal cedar tree to draw. There is camping here and at Milsap Bar.

At Milsap the water of the Feather River looks invitingly cool on a hot summer day as it flows around great granite boulders and churns down the canyon.

Cascade Saloon,
Cascade, Plumas County

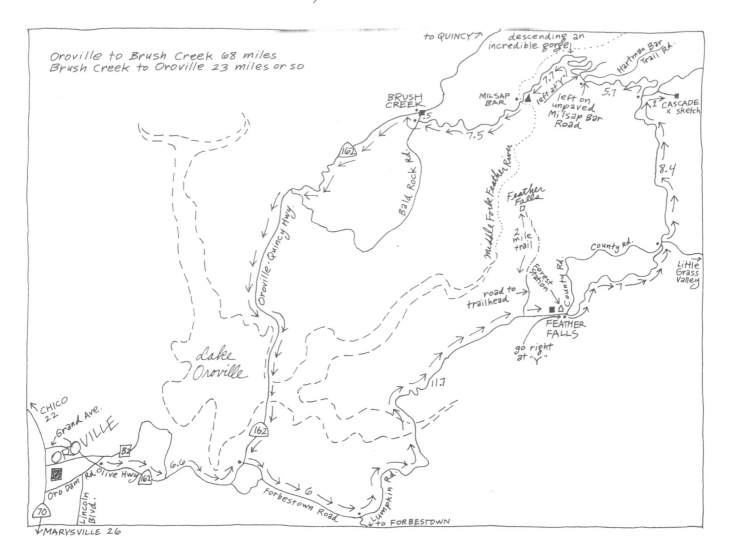

Oroville to Brush Creek 68 miles
Brush Creek to Oroville 23 miles or so

to QUINCY ↗

descending an incredible gorge

Hartman Bar Trail Rd.

7.7

left at "Y"

5.7

1 CASCADE × sketch

BRUSH CREEK ■5

MILSAP BAR ▲

left on unpaved Milsap Bar Road

162

7.5

8.4

Bald Rock Rd.

Middle Fork Feather River

Feather Falls ▯

County Rd.

Oroville-Quincy Hwy.

2 mile trail

Forest Station

County Rd.

7

Little Grass Valley

road to trailhead

Lake Oroville

FEATHER FALLS ■ ▲

go right at "Y"

↑ CHICO 22

Grand Ave.

OROVILLE

11.7

B2

Oro Dam Rd. Olive Hwy 162

6.6

162

Lincoln Blvd.

70

6

Forbestown Road

Lumpkin Rd.

to FORBESTOWN

↓ MARYSVILLE 26

The Garden Highway to Marysville and Yuba City

It is easy to get onto this road by simply coming off Interstate 5 at the Garden Highway sign just north of Sacramento. You are immediately on a levee road along the Feather River. Pay no attention to an official-looking sign, "For Yuba City go back to freeway." You will get to Yuba City on the back roads.

Interesting and sometimes elegant houses line riverbanks screened by huge bushes of oleanders. There are good views of the river from time to time and of the rich farmland of the Sacramento delta region. Plums, walnuts, corn, peaches, and tomatoes are some of the crops planted. I stop along Scheiber Road to sketch one of the great farms, the "Circle S."

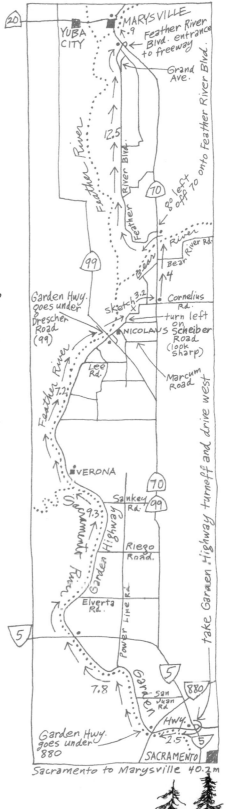

Sacramento to Marysville 40.2m

Ranch near Nicolaus, Sutter County

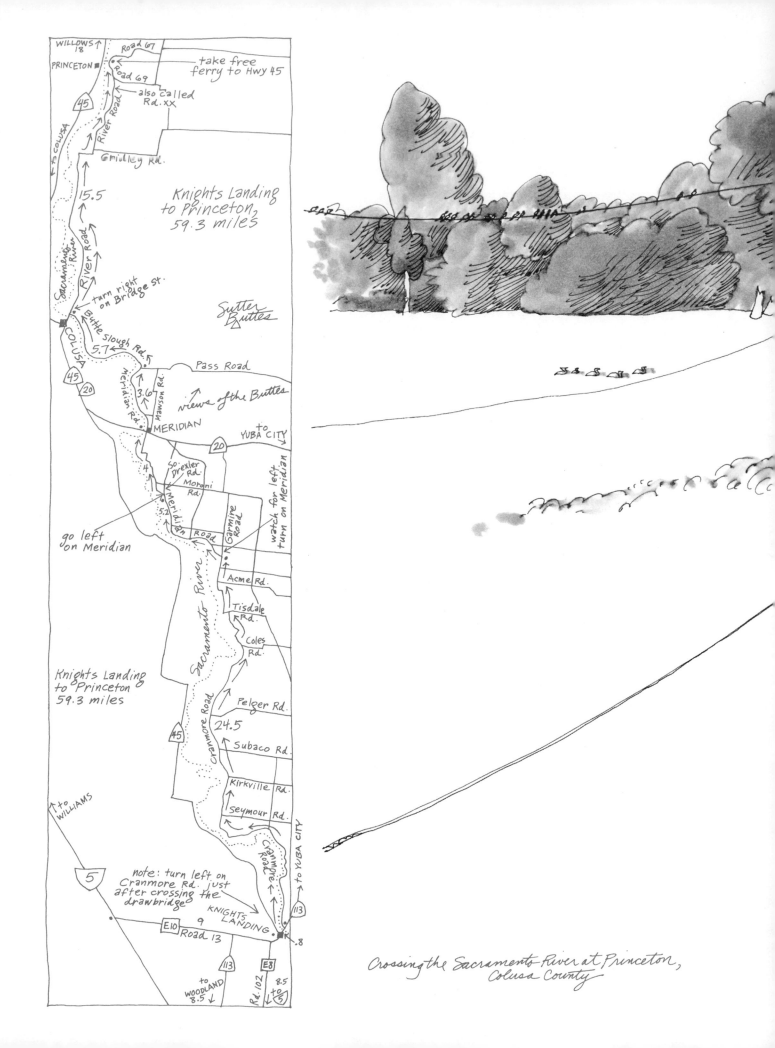

WILLOWS↑
18

Road 67

PRINCETON ■

Road 69

take free
ferry to Hwy 45

also called
Rd. xx

River Road

45

to COLUSA

Gridley Rd.

15.5

Sacramento River

River Road

Knights Landing
to Princeton,
59.3 miles

turn right
on Bridge St.

Sutter
Buttes

COLUSA

Butte Slough Rd.

5.7

45

20

Meridian Rd.

Mawson Rd.

Pass Road

3.6

views of the Buttes

MERIDIAN

to
YUBA CITY

20

So. Drexler
Rd.

4

Moroni
Rd.

Meridian Road

Garmire Road

watch for left
turn on Meridian

5.2

go left
on Meridian

Sacramento River

Acme Rd.

Tisdale
Rd.

Coles
Rd.

Knights Landing
to Princeton
59.3 miles

Cranmore Road

Pelger Rd.

45

24.5

Subaco Rd.

Kirkville Rd.

↑to
WILLIAMS

Seymour Rd.

Cranmore Road

to YUBA CITY

5

note: turn left on
Cranmore Rd. just
after crossing the
drawbridge

KNIGHTS
LANDING

113

E10
Road 13

9

.8

113

E8

to
WOODLAND
8.5 ↓

Rd. 102

8.5

to
5

*Crossing the Sacramento River at Princeton,
Colusa County*

Knights Landing to
Princeton Ferry along
the Sacramento River

Knights Landing, where scenes
were filmed around 1929 for
the movie SHOWBOAT, begins
this drive along the levee
roads of the Sacramento River.
Levee roads offer views of both
the river and agricultural land.
I watch tomatoes being harvested.
Occasionally, trucks would spill some at a
turn in the road and the blood-red squashed fruit looked
like a mortal wound in the pavement.
Blue and white herons watch me pass. Scores of
dragonflies dodge my car. Later I get a good view of
Sutter Buttes, the unusual little mountain range in the
center of the Sacramento Valley where John C.
Fremont camped in 1846. There are walnut and
peach orchards and more levees to ride on the
way to the Princeton Free Ferry.

Wheatland to Smartville

Annual grasses make up much of the vegetation in this rolling Sierra foothill country. The road passes through the Spenceville Wildlife Area, most glorious when clad in the green of spring.

Classic groves of blue, live, and valley oaks decorate the hillsides. Seated among old headstones in a hillside cemetery on McGanny Lane, I draw a view of the hamlet of Smartville. It is at Smartville that I begin to feel the atmosphere of California's gold country. The 1870 church is still the most prominent building in town and at the top of O'Brien Street is the old frame Masonic Temple.

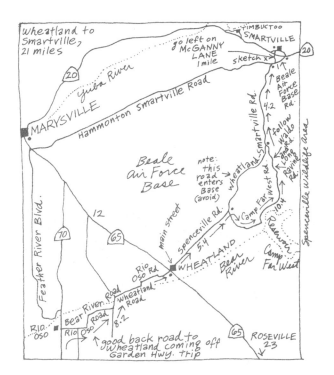

Wheatland to Smartville, 21 miles

TIMBUCTOO
SMARTVILLE
go left on McGANNY LANE 1 mile
sketch x
Beale Air Force Base Rd.
20
4.2
follow Waldo
2nd Rd. Long Ravine Rd.
Yuba River
MARYSVILLE
Hammonton Smartville Road
Wheatland-Smartville Rd.
Beale Air Force Base
note: this road enters Base (avoid)
10.4
Camp Far West Rd.
Reservoir
Spenceville Wildlife Area
Feather River Blvd.
12
main street
Spenceville Rd.
5.4
Camp Far West
70
65
Rio Oso Rd.
WHEATLAND
Bear River
Camp Far West
Bear River Road
Wheatland Road
8.1
RIO OSO
Rio Oso Road
good back road to Wheatland coming off Garden Hwy. trip
65
ROSEVILLE 23

View of Smartville, Yuba County

MARY KERRIGAN
AGE
66 YRS.
THOMAS
AGED 26 YRS.
PATRICK
AGED 5? YRS.

PETER KERRIGAN
Native
Co. Sligo
Ireland
Died Aug.
1873
Ambrose
Aged 1 day

MARY
wife of
Cornelius Denelve
died
June 7 1872.
Aged 28 years.

111

Roundabout to Nevada City

Bitney Springs Road winds through the hills above the active, growing town of Grass Valley. At Bridgeport is the longest covered bridge (233 feet) in America. It spans the South Fork of the Yuba River. In 1862, when the bridge was erected, Bridgeport was a prosperous river mining town.

At French Corral I sketch the old 1850 Wells Fargo Express Office. Today a lone goat grazes alongside the iron-doored, shuttered office that once guarded millions of dollars in gold.

FRENCH CORRAL

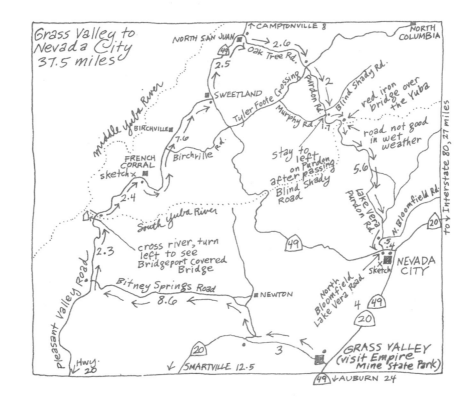

Grass Valley to
Nevada City
37.5 miles

CAMPTONVILLE 8

NORTH COLUMBIA

NORTH SAN JUAN

2.6

Oak Tree Rd.

2.5

Middle Yuba River

SWEETLAND

Tyler Foote Crossing

Murphy Rd.

Purdon Rd.

Blind Shady Rd.

red iron bridge over the Yuba

road not good in wet weather

BIRCHVILLE

7.6

Birchville Rd.

stay to left on Purdon after passing Blind Shady Road

5.6

FRENCH CORRAL
sketch x

2.4

South Yuba River

cross river, turn left to see Bridgeport Covered Bridge

Lake Vera Purdon Rd.

N. Bloomfield Rd.

to Interstate 80, 27 miles

20

Pleasant Valley Road

2.3

Bitney Springs Road

8.6

NEWTON

.5

.4

49

North Bloomfield Lake Vera Road

x sketch

NEVADA CITY

Hwy. 20

20

SMARTVILLE 12.5

3

4 49

20

GRASS VALLEY
(visit Empire Mine State Park)

49 ↓ AUBURN 24

The first settler here was, as you might suppose, a
Frenchman who built a corral for his mules in 1849.
There is little left to suggest the large, active
mining community that grew here soon after
the discovery of gold in the area.
        The road to Purdon Crossing over the South
Yuba River wouldn't be one to take in wet
weather. I travel it at 10 miles per hour
and cross the boulder-strewn Yuba on an
old, but decorative, red iron bridge.

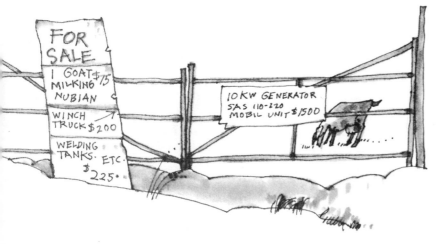

FOR SALE
1 GOAT $75
MILKING
NUBIAN

WINCH
TRUCK $200

WELDING
TANKS. ETC.
$225

10 KW GENERATOR
SAS 110-220
MOBIL UNIT $1500

French Corral, Nevada County

In Nevada City there is much to draw of historical interest. I choose to draw the more than 100-year-old Mulloy house. It still stands proudly at the head of — and as you will discover — in the middle of Broad Street. Mulloy had been part owner of the Nevada Gazette, as well as a grocer, a Justice of the Peace, and a county supervisor.

The house on Broad Street, Nevada City, Nevada County

At Malakoff Diggins, before reaching North Bloomfield, I view the multicolored, pinnacled minarets of earth left by man's attempt to wash away mountains for gold. In the 1870s hydraulic mining was used to find gold that panning, cradles, and long toms couldn't uncover.

Malakoff Diggins, Nevada County

Farmers objected to all the debris carried downstream by the ruthless procedure, and in 1884 — in a court case that received wide attention — Judge Lorenzo Sawyer handed down a ruling that would control future hydraulic mining in California. Millions of dollars in gold undoubtedly still lie in those mountains.

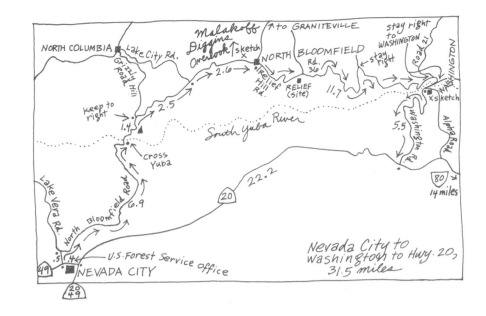

Nevada City to
Washington to Hwy. 20,
31.5 miles

North Bloomfield is a shaded community of old, well-kept houses and historic buildings, maintained by the Park Service. At Washington I sketch the general store. I notice three small hotels here and a restaurant, and I learn that the siren atop the general store goes off on Mondays at noon (unless the siren person forgets).

General store, Washington, Nevada County

North Bloomfield to Graniteville and across the Sierras
(map, page 122)

. Graniteville, at 4,900 feet elevation, is in the High Sierras. Gold was mined in gulches here as far back as 1850, but after 1883 its existence depended on quartz mining and lumbering. Today it is a peaceful community where residents appreciate a quiet and simple life in a remote and beautiful place. I stop to draw and to talk to the owners of the 1859 house that had been the residence of the local judge.

A cedar and a ponderosa pine, planted in front in 1895, have since grown to dwarf the old house. Very few trees were here at that time because the lumber of the area had been used up for housing and mine timber.

The only road going east out of Graniteville takes me to Bowman Lake, Jackson Meadow Reservoir, and, finally, to Highway 89. I realize I have crossed the mighty Sierras on a back road!

The Judge's Place, Graniteville, Nevada County

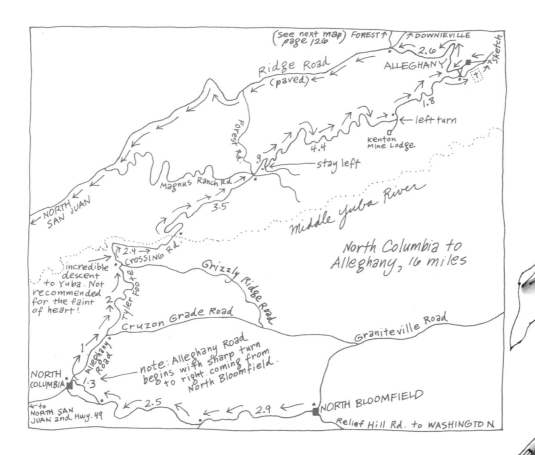

Map 1 (top):

North Bloomfield to Graniteville and across the Sierras

North Bloomfield to Hwy. 89, 43.2 miles

Pinoli Ridge Rd.

Turn right at "T" in road
Henness Pass Road

SIERRAVILLE 8.5

Jackson Meadows Road

Jackson Creek Camp

Jackson Meadow Reservoir

17.3

89 to TRUCKEE 17 ↓

Webber Lake

Sketch Road 19N14

4

GRANITEVILLE

10.8

Bowman Lake

Tahoe National Forest

3.5

4.6

1.5 ← keep to right

1.5

NORTH BLOOMFIELD

← to NEVADA CITY 19

Relief Hill Road

↓ to WASHINGTON

Map 2 (middle):

(see next map page 126) FOREST ↑   ↑ DOWNIEVILLE

2.6

Ridge Road (paved) ←

ALLEGHANY

Sketch

1.8

← left turn

4.4

Kenton Mine Lodge

Forest Rd.

.9 ← stay left

Magnus Ranch Rd.

3.5

← NORTH SAN JUAN

Middle Yuba River

North Columbia to Alleghany, 16 miles

2.4 → Crossing Rd.

incredible descent to Yuba. Not recommended for the faint of heart!

2

Tyler Foote Rd.

Grizzly Ridge Road

Cruzon Grade Road

Graniteville Road

1

Alleghany Road

NORTH COLUMBIA

1.3

note: Alleghany Road begins with sharp turn to right, coming from North Bloomfield.

← to NORTH SAN JUAN and Hwy. 49

2.5

2.9

NORTH BLOOMFIELD

Relief Hill Rd. to WASHINGTON

North Columbia to Alleghany back road

I pick the old A.D. Foote toll road to reach Alleghany. It seems incredible that men would build such a road, hewn out of rock and threading its way along a nearly perpendicular canyon wall. At several turns, walls of dry masonry are observed supporting sections of precipitous roadway.

At the beginning of the journey it is somewhat intimidating to find a sign, "Narrow road, no turnouts, one lane, last turnaround." I make it, however, sometimes at a bumpy 5 miles per hour. I ford the Yuba at Footes Crossing, drive on for big views of canyons and mountains, and eventually reach the High Sierra town of Alleghany. It is strung out along the mountainside in picturesque fashion. I sit to draw the tiny fire department in this colorful town of shiny, sloping metal roofs. From here it is easy to return to Highway 49 for the road is paved and there are more good views of forests and mountains to enjoy. This is the old Henness Pass Road, the main emigrant trail in 1849 leading from Virginia City, Nevada, to Marysville.

alleghany Fire Department

Alleghany to Forest, Camptonville or Downieville

In the middle 1850s Forest was a lively mining camp. When it became a town it was named for a Mrs. Mooney, a newspaperwoman with the unlikely first name of Forest. She signed her journalistic efforts, "Forest City."

I arrive in Forest to find a small, quiet alpine community. Opposite the Ruby Mine Office, operators of nearby gold mines, I sit under an apple tree to draw. Behind the office, in the gully, is the entrance to a caved-in mining tunnel. When miles of tunnels were being worked here, one could go all the way to Alleghany without worrying about the winter snow. Forest and Alleghany were connected by all the mining tunnels!

RUBY MINE OFFICE

House at Forest, Sierra County

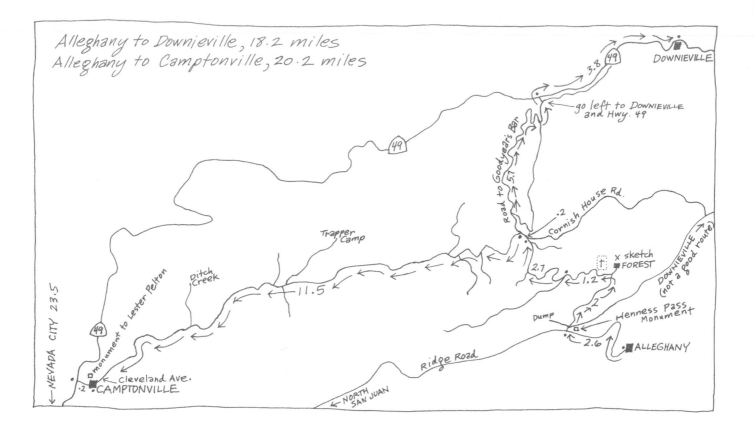

Alleghany to Downieville, 18.2 miles
Alleghany to Camptonville, 20.2 miles

DOWNIEVILLE

3.8
49

go left to DOWNIEVILLE
and Hwy. 49

49

Road to Goodyear's Bar

5.7

Cornish House Rd.

.2

Trapper Camp

2.7

x sketch
FOREST

1.2

DOWNIEVILLE (not a good route)

.2

Ditch Creek

11.5

monument to Lester Pelton

Dump

Henness Pass Monument

2.6

ALLEGHANY

NEVADA CITY 23.5

49

Cleveland Ave.

.2 CAMPTONVILLE

Ridge Road

NORTH SAN JUAN

    I then travel to the charming, historic town of
Downieville via Goodyear's Bar, a winding mountain
road, narrow, steep, and rough. I get a strong
impression of the tremendous dimension and
depth of these canyons of the High Sierras.
    An easier route, yet with grand mountain views,
is the road to Camptonville. Named for a blacksmith,
Robert Campton, the little town is noted as the place
where Lester Pelton invented the Pelton
Water Wheel in 1878.

Back road, Mourning Dove,
Sierra County

127

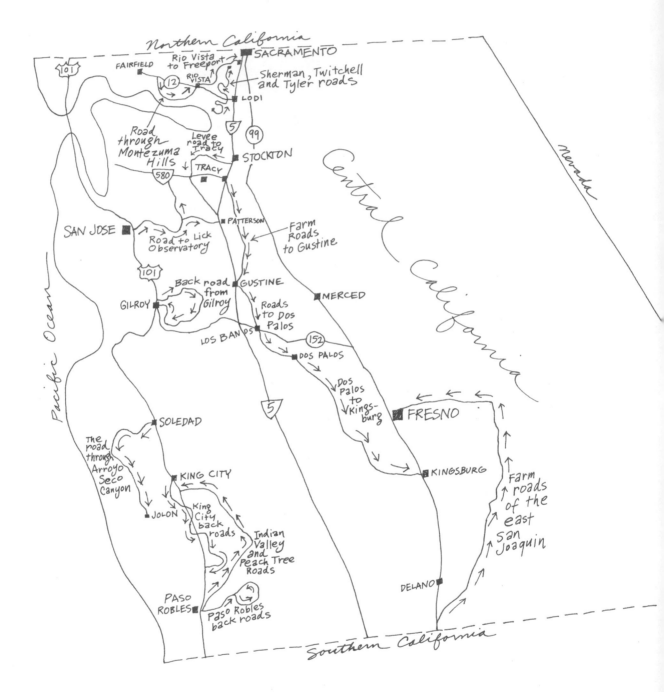

Eucalyptus, Santa Cruz County

Central California

With some good maps and an extra bit of time,
I set off — still with a sense of adventure
in taking a back route and coming upon
    the unexpected.
        I believe we all need to express
our appreciation of beauty. What better
    way to fulfill this need than by
getting closer to nature on the
        back roads.

The road through Montezuma Hills (map, page 133)

Along Shiloh Road the land is rolling. Occasional eucalyptus trees bend in the wind. I pass through Birds Landing, a shipping point for hay and wheat in the 1870s. The old Benjamin Store (1875) still stands. Almost forgotten, Collinsville hamlet slumbers at the river's edge, where the San Joaquin joins the Sacramento. The handsome profile of Mount Diablo is outlined across the water. Long ago Collinsville was a salmon fishing village. The many fishermen from Italy who worked in the cannery lived in houses built on stilts to allow flood tides to pass beneath. The town was referred to as "Little Venice."

Farm near Birds Landing, Solano County

Cows, sheep, flocks of crows, hawks, lonely farms, and lonelier windmills are seen while driving through the Montezuma Hills from Birds Landing.

The road to Rio Vista curves among the summer golden hills of Montezuma.

In town, at the corner of California and 4th streets, I draw St. Joseph's Church, built in 1868. It is surrounded by concrete painted green. From where I sketch the concrete looks like grass.

St. Joseph's Church, Rio Vista, Solano County

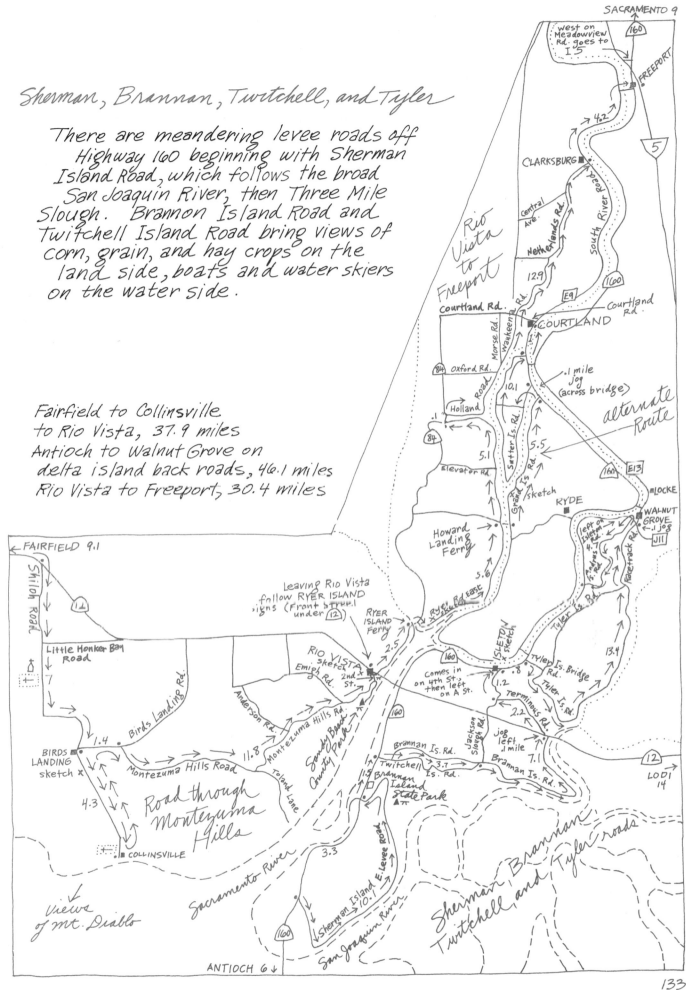

Sherman, Brannan, Twitchell, and Tyler

There are meandering levee roads off Highway 160 beginning with Sherman Island Road, which follows the broad San Joaquin River, then Three Mile Slough. Brannon Island Road and Twitchell Island Road bring views of corn, grain, and hay crops on the land side, boats and water skiers on the water side.

Fairfield to Collinsville to Rio Vista, 37.9 miles
Antioch to Walnut Grove on delta island back roads, 46.1 miles
Rio Vista to Freeport, 30.4 miles

SACRAMENTO 9

160

west on Meadowview Rd. goes to I 5

FREEPORT

4.2

5

CLARKSBURG

Central Ave.

Netherlands Rd.

South River Road

Rio Vista to Freeport

12.9

E9

160

Courtland Rd.

Courtland Rd.

COURTLAND

Waukeena Rd.

Morse Rd.

.1

84 Oxford Rd.

Holland Road

10.1

.1 mile jog (across bridge)

alternate Route

84

5.1

Sutter Is. Rd.

5.5

Elevator Rd.

Grand Is. Rd.

sketch

160

E13

RYDE

LOCKE

WALNUT GROVE

.1 jog

J11

Howard Landing Ferry

5.6

left on Isleton Rd.

St. Andrews Rd.

Racetrack Rd.

FAIRFIELD 9.1

Shiloh Road

12

Little Honker Bay Road

7

Leaving Rio Vista follow RYER ISLAND signs (Front Street under 12)

RYER ISLAND Ferry

"Ryer" Rd. sketch EAST

Tyler Is. Rd.

13.4

RIO VISTA sketch

2nd St.

2.5

160

ISLETON x sketch

Tyler Is. Bridge Rd.

Emigh Rd.

Comes in on 4th St. then left on A St.

1.2

Tyler Is. Rd.

Anderson Rd.

Montezuma Hills Rd.

Sandy Beach County Park

160

Terminus Rd.

2.2

12

LODI 14

1.4

Birds Landing Rd.

11.8

Toland Lane

Brannan Is. Rd.

Twitchell Is. Rd.

3.7

Jackson Slough Rd.

jog left .1 mile

Brannan Is. Rd.

7.1

BIRDS LANDING sketch x

Montezuma Hills Road

1.5

Brannan Island State Park

4.3

Road through Montezuma Hills

COLLINSVILLE

Sacramento River

3.3

Sherman Island E. Levee Road

10.1

San Joaquin River

Sherman, Brannan, Twitchell, and Tyler roads

views of mt. Diablo

160

ANTIOCH 6

City Hall, Isleton, Solano County

The towering dredge moored at Isleton is the town's most prominent feature. I sketch the City Hall as the siren blows and volunteer firemen rush to duty adjusting their suspenders as they go. A small town is not without drama. I complete my meandering with a drive around Tyler Island, which brings me again to Highway 160

Rio Vista to Clarksburg and Freeport (map, page 133)

I find Rio Vista a clean, pleasant riverside town.
An attractive marina is nearby and a county park for
camping and picnicking along the Sacramento River.
   I stopped to see the Dutra Museum of Dredging.
The Dutra family have made their lovely 1907 house
into a comprehensive and significant presentation
of the history of dredging in the Delta region.
   I sketch a huge bucket used on the dredge
Tule King, constructed in 1910. Its 25,000 pounds
tower over the family cat in the Dutra backyard.
   Phone 707-374-5015 for an appointment to see the
museum.

Tule King dredge bucket, Rio Vista,
Solano County

Going north I ride the free ferry to Ryer Island and sketch a well-proportioned sailboat docked in Hidden Harbor.

The day is quiet and bird sounds predominate. Geese pose in the water. A commercial crayfisherman speaks to me. His 150 traps are inspected daily in the warm summer months. One sardine and a can of dogfood are used as bait in each trap. His take in one trap can be anywhere from one to one hundred crayfish. Once hauled in, the crayfish are frozen and shipped to Sweden, where they are most particularly relished.

Delta boat, Ryer Island, Sacramento County.

An alternate route, Rio Vista to Courtland and Freeport
(map, page 133)

This road differs from the previous road in that a second free ferry at Howard Landing takes you onto Grand Island, then north again toward Freeport. Along this route, Sutter Island and Merritt Island are also traversed. On Grand Island I draw a fine Victorian house along Steamboat Slough.

House on Steamboat Slough, Yolo County

I ride the levees, eventually arriving in Freeport,
once a major shipping center for the gold mines.
A.J. Bump built the first general store/saloon in town
in 1863. It is still there when I arrive on a warm
summer day in July; a cool drink at the colorful,
old saloon tastes good. (map, page 133)

Levee road to Tracy

Strange as it seems, there are numerous islands right in the center of California. Flood plains of the Sacramento and San Joaquin rivers, reclaimed over the years for agriculture, created the many islands.
Riding levee roads requires a sharp eye all around. The levees give a command position for appreciating the waterways and the special look of island agriculture.
I sketch a historic country schoolhouse off Inland Road. It was built in 1904 and abandoned in 1946.

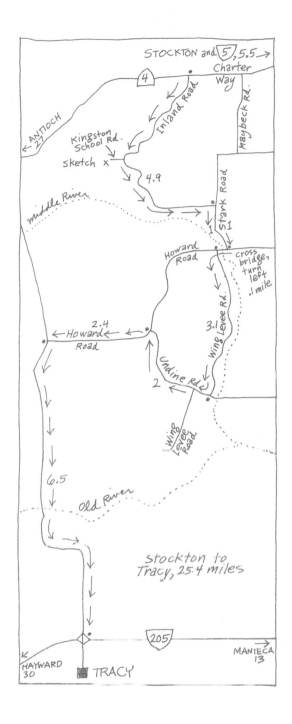

STOCKTON and 5, 5.5 →
Charter Way

4

ANTIOCH 27

Inland Road

Kingston School Rd.

sketch X

4.9

Maybeck Rd.

Stark Road

middle River

1 | 1
Stark Road

Howard Road

cross bridge, turn left .1 mile

Wing Levee Rd.

3.1

2.4
← Howard ← Road

Undine Rd.

2

Wing Levee Road

6.5

Old River

stockton to Tracy, 25.4 miles

205

K
HAYWARD 30

TRACY

MANTECA 13

Kingston School,
San Joaquin County

141

The road
to Lick
Observatory
and San Antonio
Valley

It is a windy day and overcast with thick, dark clouds.
The still green hills have begun to turn brown in some
areas. Wildflowers are cheerful spots of color on this
gray day. I stop to draw a view of Lick Observatory—
framed with oaks—visible along the ridge of Mount
Hamilton. As I drive the winding road, ground squirrels
scurry back and forth to their burrows in the bases of
ancient oak trees. You can see the mighty 120"
telescope any day of the week, and from one to five p.m. a
film may be seen at the Visitors' Center.

Lick Observatory, Mount Hamilton, Santa Clara County

It is 50 miles from here to Livermore on Lick Observatory Road, which winds down the east side of Mount Hamilton and through the lovely oak meadows of San Antonio Valley. Here the road divides, going north to Livermore and east to Patterson.

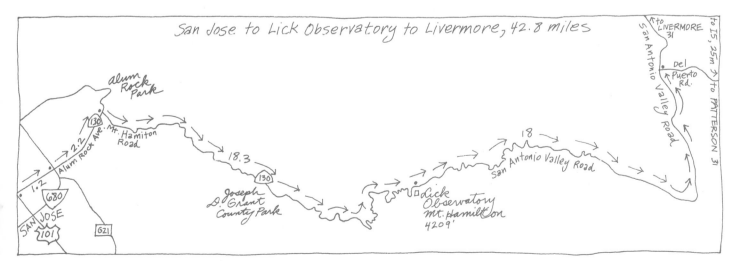

San Jose to Lick Observatory to Livermore, 42.8 miles

Back road from Gilroy

The town of Gilroy was named
for John Gilroy, soapmaker and
millwright. He had married the
daughter of Ygnacio Ortega, owner
of Rancho San Ysidro, and was given part
of the Rancho (4,460 acres) when Ygnacio
died in 1833.

La Canada Ranch, near Gilroy,
Santa Clara County

145

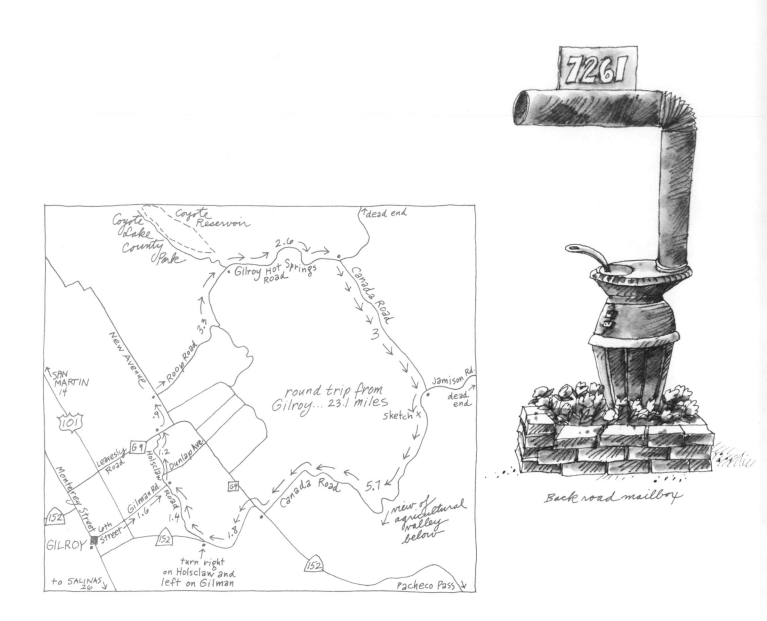

Within the map:

Coyote Lake County Park

Coyote Reservoir

↑dead end

2.6

Gilroy Hot Springs Road

Canada Road

3

New Avenue

Rooly Road 3.3

SAN MARTIN 14

round trip from Gilroy... 23.1 miles

Jamison Rd.
dead end

sketch ×

101

Leavesly Road

G9

1.2

Dunlap Ave.

Holsclaw Road

.9

Monterey Street

6th Street

Gilman Rd.

1.6

G9

Canada Road

5.7

152

152

1.4

1.8

view of agricultural valley below

GILROY

turn right on Holsclaw and left on Gilman

152

to SALINAS 26

Pacheco Pass

Back road mailbox

John was influential enough for the present town
of Gilroy to be named for him; however, in 1869 he died
in poverty, aged 73 years. It is interesting that his
name was really Cameron. Gilroy was his mother's
maiden name, which he took when he deserted
ship at Monterey in 1814 so as not to be traced.
    I sketch a scene along Canada Road, a ranch
nestled at the base of sloping hills. Poppies, mustard,
and purple vetch bloom on this bright spring day.
    I watch a bobcat warily cross the road
    and bound through grass and flowers.

The road through Arroyo Seco Canyon

I see the harvesting of lettuce on my way. A huge motorized sprinkler creeps over the planted landscape of cabbage, onions, and grape crops! One large unplanted field is orange with poppies.

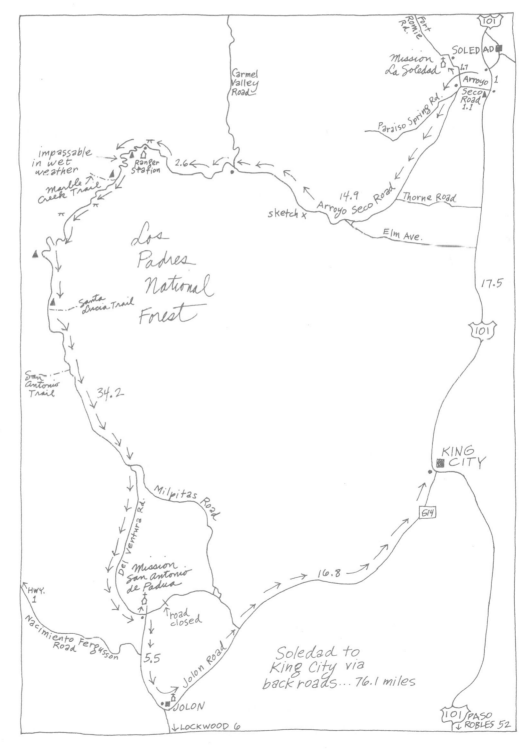

I draw a white barn and the complex canyon walls of Arroyo Seco, while the ranch dog returns a large rock for me to throw again and again.

Gould Ranch, Arroyo Seco Canyon, Monterey County

148

It is April, and with forest fires unlikely and the temperature comfortable, an ideal time to travel this colorful road. The road ends at Mission San Antonio de Padua, founded in 1771 and one of the most picturesque of the California missions. It stands in the valley of the San Antonio River and had been well known for its high quality wheat and fine horses.

The road narrows in Los Padres National Forest and winds along mountain ledges. Yucca blooms in creamy white splendor, and firewood, ceanothus, monkey flower, paintbrush, and yerba santa color the roadside.

Grapevine in May, near King City,
Monterey County

King City back roads

On Oasis Road I see thousands of grapevines patterning the hills and dales south of King City. They are all marked, cordoned, and prepared for mechanical harvesting. I draw an Early Burgundy varietal at the flowering stage when young grape bunches are just beginning. A sprinkling device is attached to this grape stake. An airplane is dusting other vineyards in the vicinity with sulphur, but I am lucky to be distant enough from this activity.

The roads parallel Highway 101 and I find myself south of San Ardo surrounded by a forest of oil pump jacks. I hold my nose and clear this area as I proceed inland on Sargeants Valley Road. Brown rolling hills and golden grain fields fill the landscape.

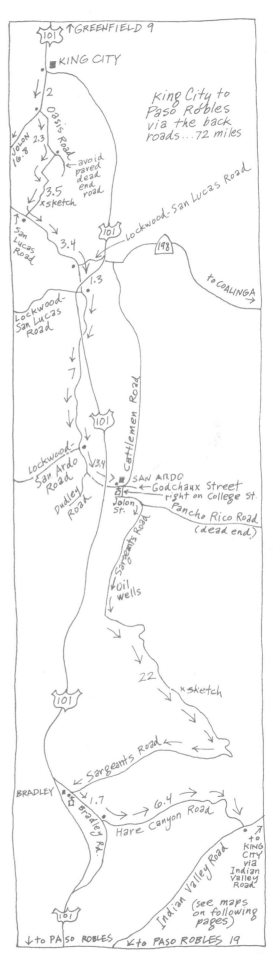

King City to Paso Robles via the back roads... 72 miles

101 ↑GREENFIELD 9

KING CITY

2

Jolon 16.8

Oasis Road

2.3

avoid paved dead end road

3.5 ×sketch

San Lucas Road

101

Lockwood-San Lucas Road

198

3.4

to COALINGA

1.3

Lockwood-San Lucas Road

7

101

Lockwood-San Ardo Road

Cattlemen Road

↓3.4

SAN ARDO

Dudley Road

Godchaux Street right on College St.

Jolon St.

Pancho Rico Road (dead end)

Sargeants Road

↓oil wells

22 ×sketch

101

Sargeants Road

BRADLEY

1.7

6.4

Hare Canyon Road

Bradley Rd.

Indian Valley Road

↗ to KING CITY via Indian Valley Road

(see maps on following pages)

101

↓to PASO ROBLES   ↓to PASO ROBLES 19

151

I stop to draw a Pinto horse—
an inspired design for a
mailbox made of welded steel
parts.   You can return to
Highway 101 at Bradley or
take Hare Canyon Road
and Indian Valley Road to
King City or Paso Robles.

Pinto mailbox, near Bradley, Monterey County

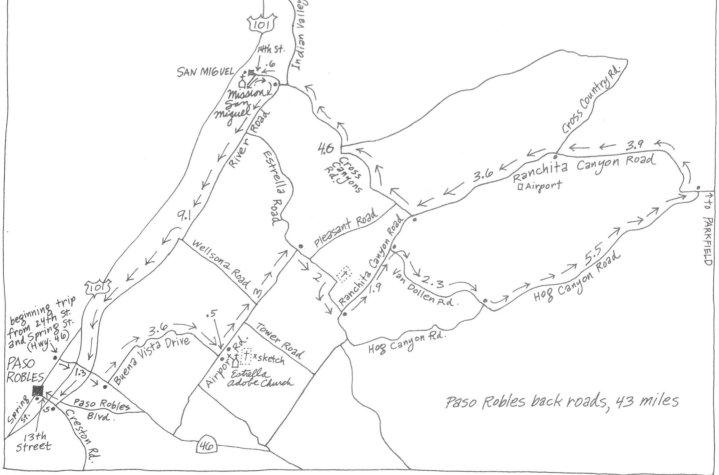

Paso Robles back roads, 43 miles

Paso Robles back roads

On the plains of Estrella, in 1879, Christian pioneers built Estrella Adobe Church. It was restored in 1952 and part of the cemetery was saved. From the grave markers, I am able to piece together the heart-tugging story of the Stovall family: Little Albert, the youngest, whose headstone reads "Born May 13, 1881, son died May 4, 1885

Twas our laughing blue eyed Boy
Our comfort and our household joy
Over the river he beckons to me
The gates of the city we
   cannot see";
then the middle son Walter M. (September 8, 1875 – May 23, 1885); mother Mary C. (died March 15, 1905, 63 years 18 days); and father F.M. (died August 16, 1907, 64 years/1 mo./18 dys.).

Evan P.'s marker is pictured here. Sentimental verse has its effect on me!

Roads wind around here and over rolling hills textured with grain, hay crops, and vineyards. A large hawk poses on a fencepost.

I stop to explore Mission San Miguel Archangel, a lovely old church founded in 1797, and then return to Paso Robles on River Road.

EVAN P.
SON OF
F. M. & M. C.
STOVALL
BORN
OCT. 30, 1878
DIED
JUNE 15, 1885.

The angels to Evan did whisper,
Jesus has called you away,
To join your dear Brothers in Heaven
Our darling did meekly obey.

Headstone at Estrella Adobe Church graveyard, near Paso Robles, San Luis Obispo County

Indian Valley and Peach Tree roads

Along Indian Valley and Peach Tree roads, I see pleasant vistas aplenty of valleys, farms, rolling hills, majestic oaks, and pines. Shaded by a giant oak, I sketch a view of Peach Tree and Hidalgo canyons looking west into the late afternoon sun.

On Freeman Flat Road vineyards create a rolling sea of row upon row of intensely green vines.

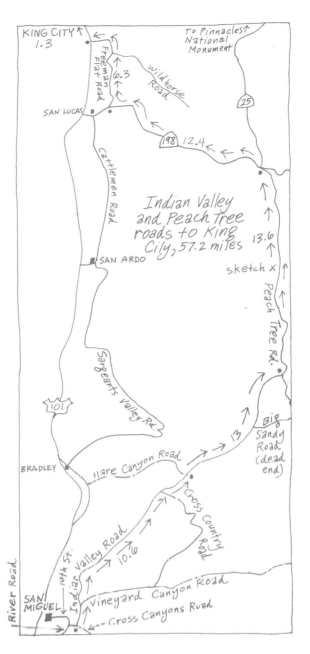

KING CITY ↑ 1.3

to Pinnacles National Monument

Freeman Flat Road

←6.3←

Wildhorse Road

25

SAN LUCAS

198 12.4←

Cattlemen Road

Indian Valley and Peach Tree roads to King City, 57.2 miles

13.6

SAN ARDO

sketch X

Peach Tree Rd.

Sargeants Valley Rd.

101

13

Big Sandy Road (dead end)

BRADLEY

Hare Canyon Road

Cross Country Road

River Road

14th St.

Indian Valley Road

10.6

SAN MIGUEL

Vineyard Canyon Road

Cross Canyons Road

Peach Tree Canyon, Monterey County

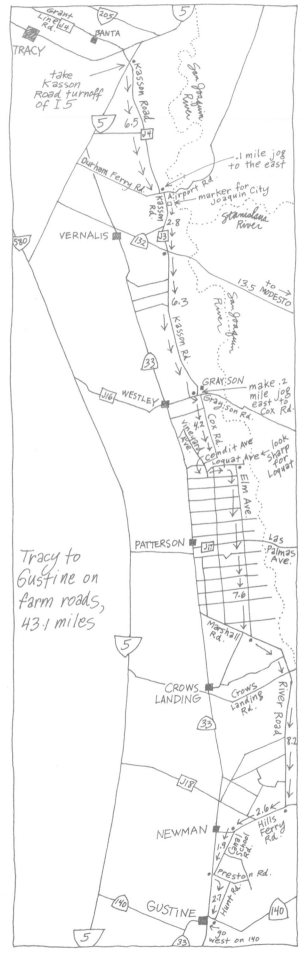

Farm roads through the San Joaquin Valley

From Tracy palm-lined Kasson Road goes south, beginning a farm road journey directly through California's greatest agricultural valley. On a clear day the snow-capped Sierras can be viewed to the east. I stop to read a marker at the site of San Joaquin City, established in 1849. In 1880 it had a hotel, warehouse, two saloons, stores, and houses. Pioneers and freight wagons crossed the river at nearby Durham Ferry. The Spanish explorer Gabriel Moraga had named this river San Joaquin in 1813.

Later, I drive around the village of Grayson, noting the many little churches. Along Elm Road I pass a unique enterprise, a turf farm.

In the pleasant town of Gustine, I sketch a small grove of orange trees along its main thoroughfare. Gustine's old-fashioned water tower is in the background. Sighting the water tower is often the first indication of a town in the offing as these farm roads proceed.

Orange trees, Gustine, Merced County

A short diversion onto Mercey Springs and Wolfsen roads brings me to San Luis Camp adobe, the oldest building in the county. It was built in 1848 by Francisco Pacheco and became a stopping place for vaqueros driving cattle to the gold fields. When land baron Henry Miller was in the area, he usually stayed here.

Further on I travel through the San Luis Wildlife Refuge. There is a herd of Tule elk in a large enclosure, where one massive-horned bull elk has corralled all the females. Other bulls stand a long way off, quite deserted and forlorn looking. Some 800 Tule elk are all that remain of the 500,000 that once roamed the grasslands of the San Joaquin Valley. Many ducks, eagles, hawks, and heron are also to be seen in the refuge.

San Luis Camp adobe, Merced County

159

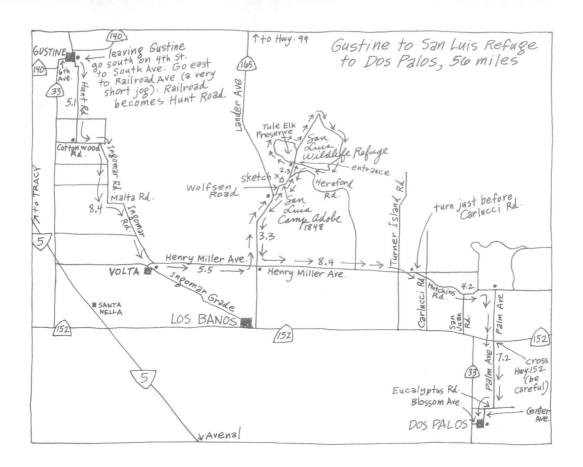

Map labels:

Gustine to San Luis Refuge to Dos Palos, 56 miles

GUSTINE

140 · 6th Ave. · 140 · 33 · Hunt Rd. · 5.1

leaving Gustine go south on 4th St. to South Ave. Go east to Railroad Ave (a very short jog). Railroad becomes Hunt Road.

↑ to Hwy. 99

165

Lander Ave.

Cottonwood Rd.

Ingomar Rd. · Malta Rd. · 8.4 · Ingomar Rd.

← to TRACY

5

152

Tule Elk Preserve

San Luis Wildlife Refuge · entrance

sketch × △ · 2.3

Wolfsen Road

Hereford Rd.

San Luis Camp Adobe 1848

3.3

Turner Island Rd.

turn just before Carlucci Rd.

Henry Miller Ave. · 5.5 → · Henry Miller Ave. · 8.4 →

VOLTA · Ingomar Grade

SANTA NELLA

LOS BANOS · 152

Carlucci Rd. · Hutchins Rd. · 4.2

San Juan Rd. · Palm Ave.

152

33 · Palm Ave. · 7.2 · cross Hwy.152 (be careful)

Eucalyptus Rd. Blossom Ave.

Center Ave.

DOS PALOS

5

↓ Avenal

Dos Palos to Kingsburg

In a small brochure called "The Fertile Fields of Dos Palos Colony," published in 1902, farmers were coaxed by landowners Miller and Lux to buy and settle here. Land was $30 to $75 per acre at 6% interest.

Beekeepers realized that in Dos Palos (Two Poles) the rich alfalfa crop aided in creating the thickest, richest, whitest honey in the world. 60,000 dozen eggs a year were produced, alfalfa sold f.o.b. at $8.50 per ton, cows sold for $45 to $60 a head.

Water tower of Dos Palos, Merced County

Two passenger trains as well as two freight trains ran every day to San Francisco, making daily newspapers available. Today Dos Palos continues as a booming agricultural town, center for a large area of diversified farming.

I sketch the new water tower, not as quaint as Gustine's.

On my trip south I see farm roads lined with wads of cotton blown from truck trailers during harvest time. Big red corn harvesters gather in a winter crop of dried corn and process it; the kernels are then loaded into trucks and carted away.

Nearing Kingsburg, I sketch in the cemetery I remember from my youth, where my mother, dad, and grandparents are buried. It is still a meticulously well-kept place. The cypress trees are even taller than I remember.

Kingsburg itself is a fine valley town with a Swedish theme to its main street (Draper Street) architecture. Reaching Kingsburg, I have now traversed a good part of the San Joaquin Valley on farm roads.

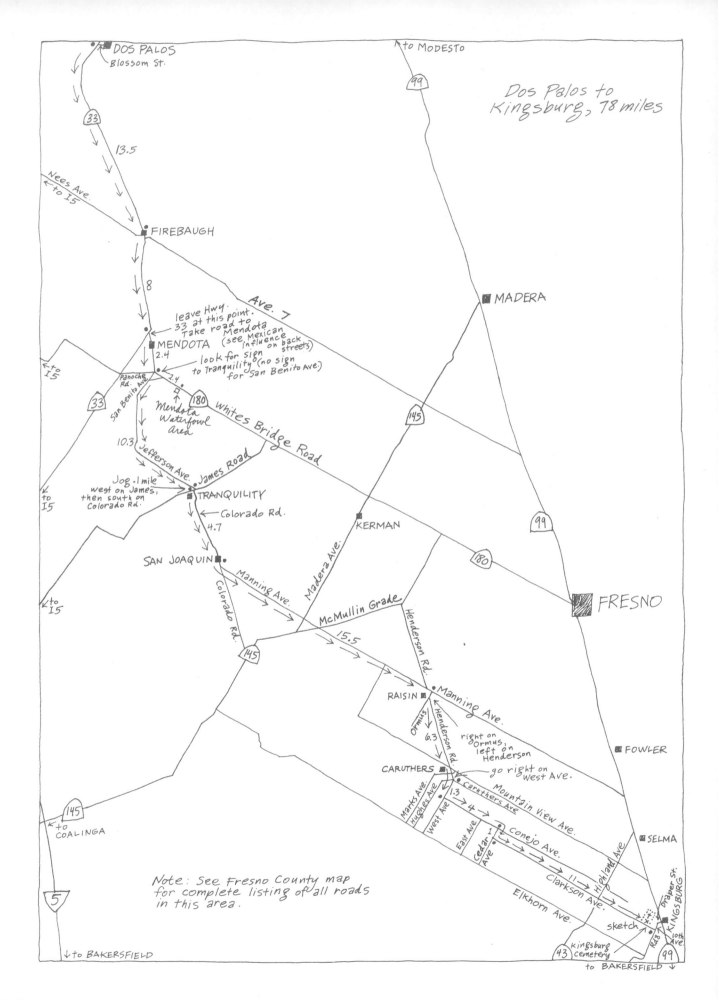

Dos Palos to
Kingsburg, 78 miles

DOS PALOS
Blossom St.

to MODESTO
99

33
13.5

Nees Ave.
to I5

FIREBAUGH
8

Ave. 7

MADERA

leave Hwy.
33 at this point.
Take road to
Mendota
(see Mexican
influence on back
streets)

MENDOTA
2.4

look for sign
to Tranquility
(no sign
for San Benito Ave.)

to I5

Panoche Rd.
San Benito Ave.
2.4

145

33

180

Mendota
Waterfowl
Area

Whites Bridge Road

10.3

Jefferson Ave.
James Road

to I5

Jog .1 mile
west on James,
then south on
Colorado Rd.

TRANQUILITY

Colorado Rd.
4.7

KERMAN

Madera Ave.

99

SAN JOAQUIN

Manning Ave.

180

Colorado Rd.

FRESNO

McMullin Grade

15.5

145

Henderson Rd.

to I5

RAISIN
Manning Ave.

Ormus

Henderson Rd.
6.3

right on
Ormus,
left on
Henderson

FOWLER

145

to COALINGA

CARUTHERS

Marks Ave.
Hughes Ave.

go right on
West Ave.

Caruthers Ave.

Mountain View Ave.

1.3
West Ave.
4

East Ave.
Cedar Ave.

Conejo Ave.
1

11

Clarkson Ave.

Highland Ave.

SELMA

Note: See Fresno County map
for complete listing of all roads
in this area.

5

Elkhorn Ave.

sketch

Draper St.
KINGSBURG
Rd 8
10th Ave.

to BAKERSFIELD

43

Kingsburg
cemetery

Rd 8

99

to BAKERSFIELD

Cypresses, Kingsburg, Fresno County

163

Farm roads of the east San Joaquin Valley

I turn off the busy highway and seek tranquil farm roads going north. I picnic at Lake Woolames on the Friant Kern Canal. Driving on, I see rice and cotton crops, and olive and walnut trees, among many other vegetable and fruit crops. It is raining today and I see cows in muddy splendor near a gigantic pile of manure.

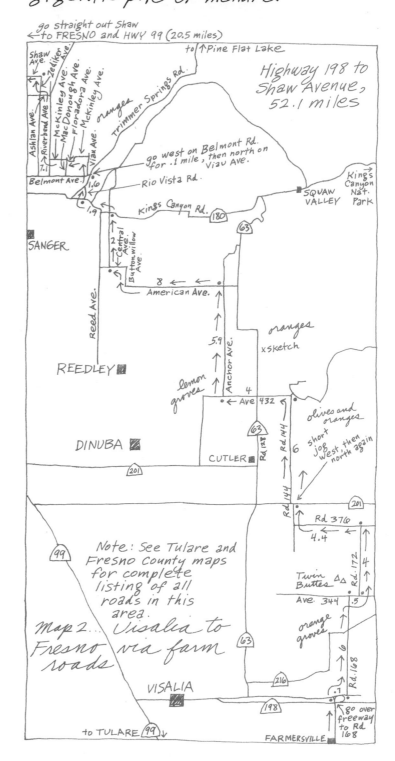

Orange groves are
dominant as I proceed
north, skirting foothills
of the Sierra Nevada mountains.
I marvel at how attractively
nature has decorated the
lush green orchard trees
with colorful oranges.

Fresno County oranges

165

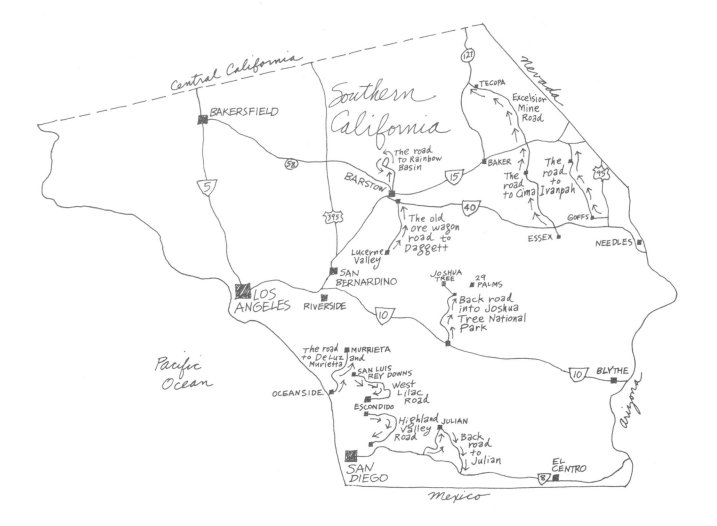

Central California

Southern California

BAKERSFIELD

121

TECOPA

Excelsior
Mine
Road

Nevada

58

5

BARSTOW

The road
to Rainbow
Basin

BAKER

15

The
road
to Cima

The
road
to
Ivanpah

95

395

40

The old
ore wagon
road to
Daggett

GOFFS

Lucerne
Valley

ESSEX

NEEDLES

SAN
BERNARDINO

JOSHUA
TREE

29
PALMS

LOS
ANGELES

RIVERSIDE

10

Back road
into Joshua
Tree National
Park

Pacific
Ocean

The road
to De Luz
Murietta

MURRIETA
and

San Luis
Rey Downs

West
Lilac
Road

10

BLYTHE

Arizona

OCEANSIDE

ESCONDIDO

Highland
Valley
Road

JULIAN

Back
road
to
Julian

SAN
DIEGO

EL
CENTRO

8

Mexico

166

Sketching helps one to see the world through fresh eyes, to see some beauty everywhere, even where it's least expected. Henry Moore said that "one draws to concentrate knowledge."
I believe that this is one of the great functions of drawing. It is a shame that more of us do not take advantage of this avenue of expression to increase our appreciation of the world.

Years ago many more artists and laymen sketched outdoors. They knew well the creative journey the pen takes in the process. The camera has now replaced the pen, I suppose, but without the same rewards.
Knowledge of a subject is not absorbed with the same thoroughness.
It doesn't take long to learn to draw fairly well and I hope you will try it!

Wind Poppy,
Santa Barbara County

The road to De Luz and Murrieta

Cattle, sheep, and horses once grazed the fields in the valley where Mission San Luis Rey de Francia is located. The church was completed in 1815. Father Peyri, for 34 years the Mission's leader, was forced to leave when a law expelling all Spaniards was passed in 1829. Restoration of the Mission occurred later, and in 1893 it was rededicated as a Franciscan seminary.

Today one must drive a way to outdistance housing and shopping developments that have sprung up in the once secluded valley.

Along North River Road and Sleeping Indian Road, farming country reappears. Strawberry fields cover entire hillsides where scores of laborers pick the fruit. Plastic coverings between the plants glisten like armor plate. Other hills are textured with citrus and avocado groves.

There are palm and eucalyptus trees, and red tile-roofed houses perch on knolls in the picturesque hills.

Between De Luz and Murrieta I stop to lunch in a grove of venerable silver-barked oaks. Near Murrieta I am honored with a clear view of the snowcapped San Bernardino and San Jacinto mountains and the broad valley below.

Oceanside to De Luz and Murrieta, 46.6 miles

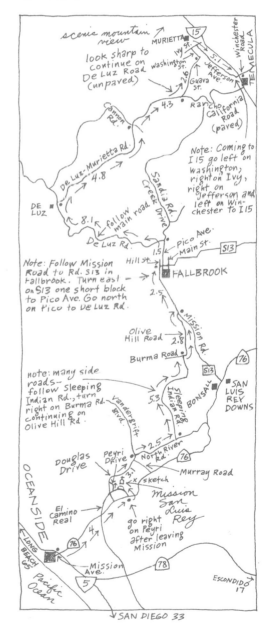

scenic mountain view
MURIETTA
15
Winchester Road
TEMECULA
look sharp to continue on De Luz Road (unpaved)
Ivy St.
5.1
Washington St.
Jefferson Ave.
Guava St.
4.3
Rancho California Road (paved)
Canyon Rd.
Note: Coming to I 15 go left on Washington, right on Ivy, right on Jefferson and left on Winchester to I 15
De Luz-Murrieta Rd.
4.8
Sandia Creek Drive
DE LUZ
8.1
follow main road
De Luz Rd.
1.5
Pico Ave.
Main St.
S13
Note: Follow Mission Road to Rd. S13 in Fallbrook. Turn east on S13 one short block to Pico Ave. Go north on Pico to De Luz Rd.
Hill St.
FALLBROOK
2.5
Mission Rd.
Olive Hill Road
2.8
Burma Road
S13
76
SAN LUIS REY DOWNS
note: many side roads—follow Sleeping Indian Rd., turn right on Burma Rd. continuing on Olive Hill Rd.
Vandergrift Blvd.
Sleeping Indian Rd.
5.3
BONSALL
2.5
North River Rd.
76
Douglas Drive
Peyri Drive
Murray Road
sketch
Mission San Luis Rey
El Camino Real
go right on Peyri after leaving Mission
OCEANSIDE
76
4
Long Beach 65
Mission Ave.
78
Pacific Ocean
5
ESCONDIDO 17
↓ SAN DIEGO 33

Mission San Luis Rey, San Diego County

West Lilac Road

West Lilac Road runs through
up-and-down hills dotted with
avocado and citrus groves. Houses
perched here and there take advantage
of the many views of surrounding
hills and orchards. Big-leafed
avocado trees make walls of green
along the winding road. And in
other orchards, oranges and lemons
look like Christmas tree ornaments
as they ripen to full color.

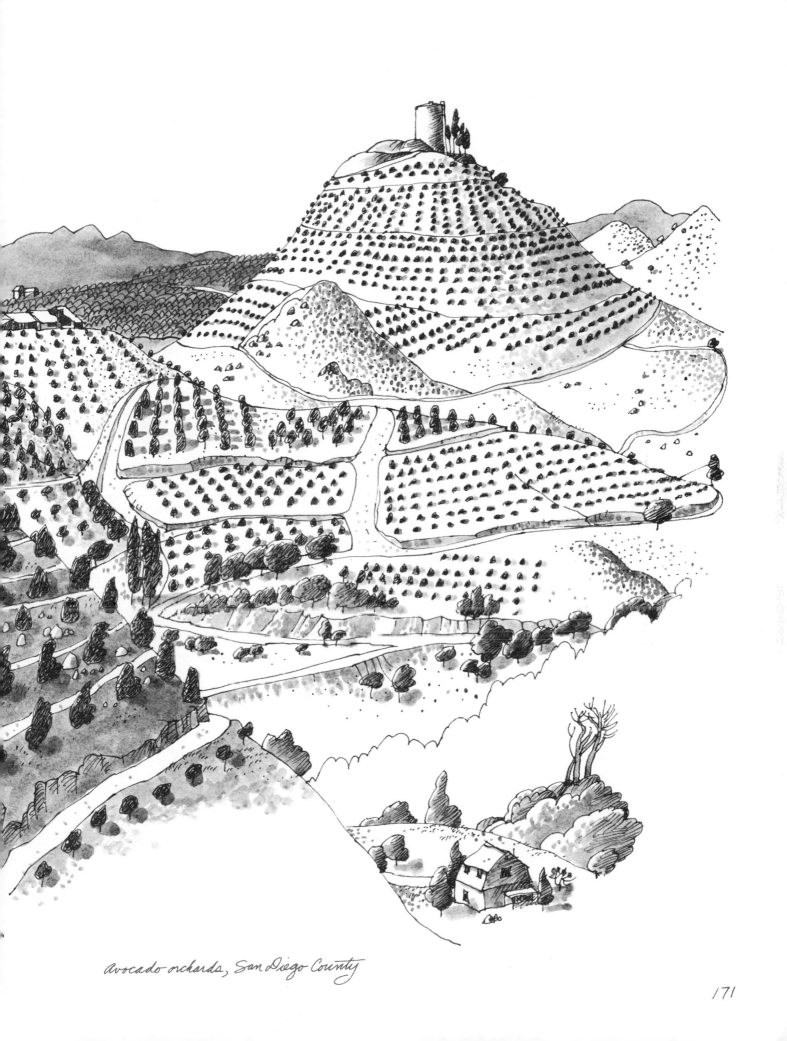

avocado orchards, San Diego County

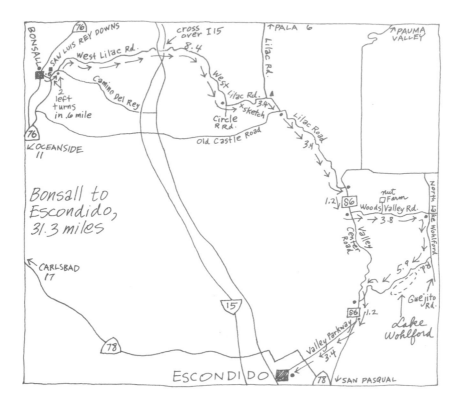

BONSALL
76 SAN LUIS REY DOWNS
cross over I15
8.4
↑PALA 6
PAUMA VALLEY
West Lilac Rd.
Camino Del Rey
2 left turns in .6 mile
Lilac Rd.
West Lilac Rd.
3.4
←sketch
Circle R Rd.
76
←OCEANSIDE 11
Old Castle Road
Lilac Road
3.4

Bonsall to Escondido, 31.3 miles

1.2 S6
nut Farm
North Lake Wohlford
Woods Valley Rd.
3.8
Valley Center Road
5.9
Guejito Rd.
←CARLSBAD 17
15
S6 1.2
Lake Wohlford
78
Valley Parkway
3.4
ESCONDIDO
78 ↓SAN PASQUAL

Highland Valley Road — map

- take Highland Road exit
- 15
- look sharp turn for left Valley Rd.
- Highland Valley Rd.
- .3
- Highland 4
- Bandy Canyon Road
- good views
- 7.1
- x sketch
- Rangeland Road
- Pomerado Road
- Archie Moore Rd.
- Highland Valley Rd. 2.4
- Ramona Street
- 67
- Warnock St.
- RAMONA
- 78
- San Vicente Rd.
- 3
- 2.2
- jog right on 67, then turn left on Dye Rd. .1 mile
- Wildcat Canyon Road
- 15
- to SAN DIEGO
- S4
- POWAY
- Barona Ranch Indian Reservation
- 7
- x sketch Barona Mission
- 67
- 8.9
- Wildcat Canyon Rd.
- Interstate 15 to Lakeside, 35.2 miles
- Willow Rd.
- .3
- Mapleview Rd.
- EL CAJON 6
- 67
- LAKESIDE

Highland Valley Road

The avocado trees in my drawing are planted strategically between colossal boulders high above San Pasqual Valley. The two elements seem to complement each other—the dark green trees and the light pink and tan rock formations.

Avocado orchard near Ramona, San Diego County

Along the mountain drive through the Barona
Indian Reservation, I stop to draw the crisply white
Indian Mission. The church has reddish-brown
trim with Christmas lights still in place. I inspect
the neat, warm interior of the little church and
the pictures on the walls. It is a pleasant place
indeed.   Wildcat Canyon soon descends
from here toward Lakeside.

Julian back road round trip

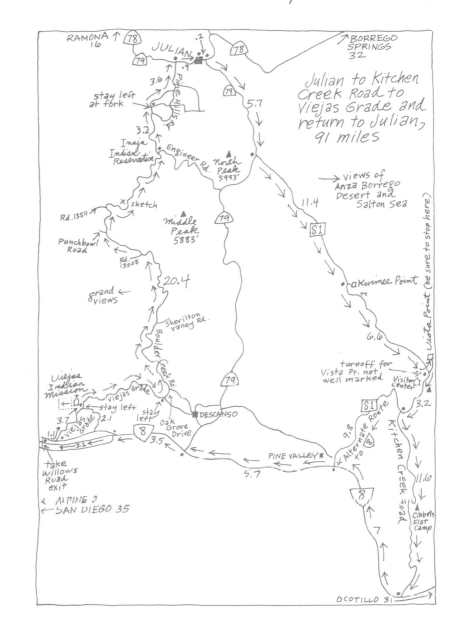

RAMONA ↑ 78   .2   ↑ BORREGO
16   JULIAN   78   SPRINGS
79   .9   32

3.6   79   5.7

stay left
at fork

3.2   Julian to Kitchen
Creek Road to
Viejas Grade and
return to Julian,
91 miles

Inaja
Indian   Engineer Rd.
Reservation   North
Peak
5993'

→ Views of
Anza Borrego
Desert and
Salton Sea

x sketch   11.4

Rd.13511   Middle   79   S1
Peak
5883'

Punchbowl
Road   Rd.
13508

20.4

grand ←
views

Sherilton   Kwimee Point
Valley Rd.

6.6

turnoff for
Vista Pt. not   Visitor
Viejas   well marked   Center
Indian
Mission   Viejas Grade   S1   3.2

stay left   stay   9.8
3.7   left   DESCANSO   Alternate Route to 4   Kitchen Creek Road
Viejas Grade 2.1   Oak Grove
Drive
1.1   8   3.5   11.6
2.2   PINE VALLEY   8

take   5.7   7   Cibbets
Willows   Flat
Road   Camp
exit

↑ ALPINE 3
← SAN DIEGO 35

OCOTILLO 31

Vista Point (be sure to stop here)

Barona Mission Church,
San Diego County

Julian back road round trip

A miner's rush to Julian in 1870 followed the discoverey of gold in the area and lasted until about 1880. Homesteaders followed the miners and fruit growing, bees, and livestock made the town a trading center. Today tourists find its historic atmosphere attractive. I begin from here and travel Highway 79 to Road S1. There are top-of-the-world views along S1 of the great and colorful Desert State Park. Row after row of beige, brown, and pink mountains fade into infinity. Later, descending into Kitchen Valley, I have long views south to the mountains of Mexico. On my return toward Julian Viejas Grade I see a long view of the valley below. Cows graze in the meadows.

I pass Blessed Virgin Mary Church with its colorful cemetery and ascend through brush and rock hills silhouetted against a bright blue sky. Ranches along the road have names like Serenity, Rockin' Chair, Expensive Spread, Fugitive Creek, and Grandpa's Mountains.

I draw a view of Cosmit Peak, which the road semicircles. It is quiet and peaceful here, with a lone circling hawk and an occasional scurrying squirrel.

"Whale" bus, seen along the back roads

*View of Cosmit Peak, Boulder Creek Road to Julian,
San Diego County*

Back road into Joshua Tree National Park

An unmarked back road near Indio heads up a brown and barren canyon that looks quite forbidding. A sign recommends that I have ample gas, oil, and water. A shacklike ranch has another sign stating that attack dogs are on duty. There are rugged, desert hills all around. Possibly this would have been a bandit hideaway in earlier times. As the canyon narrows, I consider that I wouldn't care to be here if flash flooding were a possibility. The road continues to climb. Joshua trees appear and I cross the National Park boundary. There is a sweeping view of Pleasant Valley dotted with Joshua trees.

Malapai Hill, Joshua Tree National Monument, Riverside County

I sketch the black basalt twin peaks of Malapai Hill and drive on to Squaw Tank. Should you begin this trip from within the park, pick up a brochure at the Squaw Tank turnoff of the main drive. Numbered locations are described in it to help you understand the significant geology to be seen. It may be enough, however, to simply observe the masterful arrangement of boulders (as big as houses) set one upon the other and the rich assortment of desert plants: joshuas, yuccas, needle, and cholla cactus, and many more.

The old ore wagon road to Daggett

Pink desert mountains glow in the distance as I cross a flat desert plain. I'm now traveling on Camp Rock Road, used to haul ore to Lucerne Valley or Daggett in the early days of mining. At dry Anderson Lake motor bikes are scouring up clouds of dust, and at so-called "Rimbender Camp" motor homes are arranged in a circle, like Conestoga wagons of pioneer days.

But the desert is vast and all this is forgotten in the appreciation of the purple, chocolate, and salmon-colored splendor of mountains lit by the morning sun. The desert floor is the warm olive hue of a hundred thousand creosote bushes. Coming out of the final canyon pass, I view the Calico Mountains, aptly named because of the many colors painting its peaks and canyons.

View of Ord Mountains from Camp Rock Road on the way to Daggett, San Bernardino County

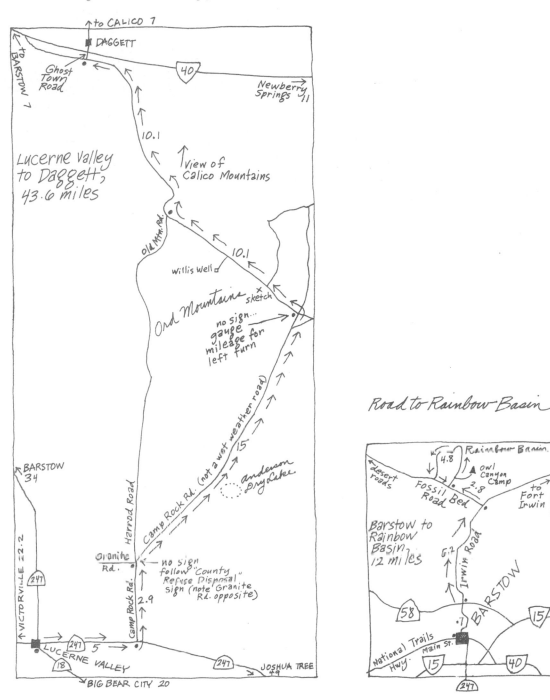

The road to Rainbow Basin

Near Barstow is Rainbow Basin Natural Area. It is a region of uplifted lake beds showing striated and patterned earth. There are variations of purple, beige, chocolate, gray, and green colors in the landscape.

The road winds through Rainbow Basin, giving good opportunities for viewing this unusual area.

Rainbow Basin landscape near Barstow, San Bernardino County

The road to Ivanpah

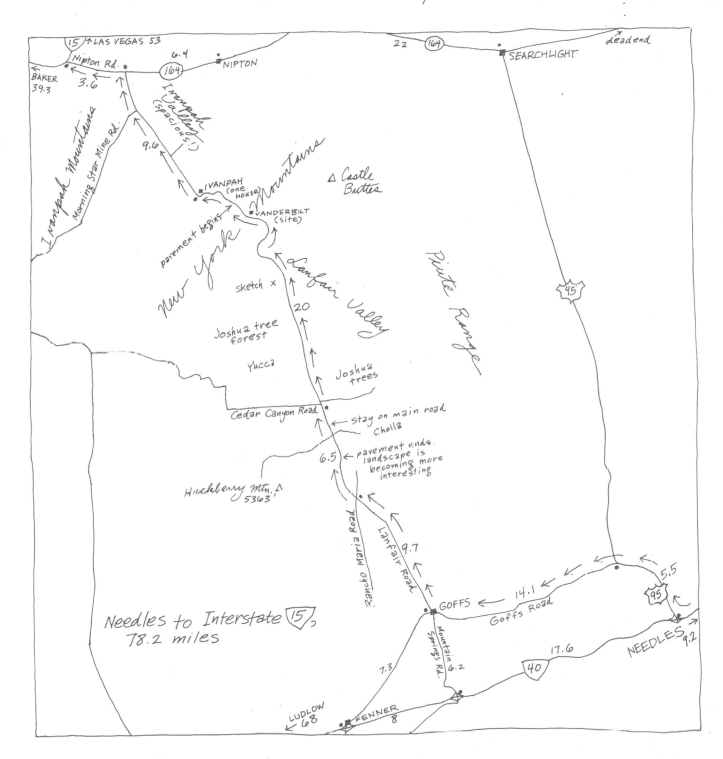

View of the New York Mountains,
Lanfair Valley, San Bernardino
County

184

The road to Ivanpah (map, page 183)

    The desert road becomes more interesting as altitude increases. Mojave yuccas and joshua trees are abundant. There are close views of Piute Range and Castle Mountains across Lanfair Valley.
    I sketch the New York Mountains, orange and tan, with mountain juniper dotting them green. The sky just above the peaks is intensely blue. It is quiet here, and I muse how few chances I have to enjoy such profound stillness. When I reach Ivanpah I find but one house near the railroad tracks, with miles and miles of desert silence all around.

Back road to Cima (map, page 186)

    I see yuccas and joshuas, forests of them, as I drive toward Cima. And chollas' spiky needles glisten in the sunshine. Range cattle with immense horns sometimes block the road.
    The low elevation of the winter sun makes deep shadows in the mountains. I pass through an area forested with juniper, the pinyon pine, then joshua trees again. It is a drive with a rich variety of desert plants to observe.

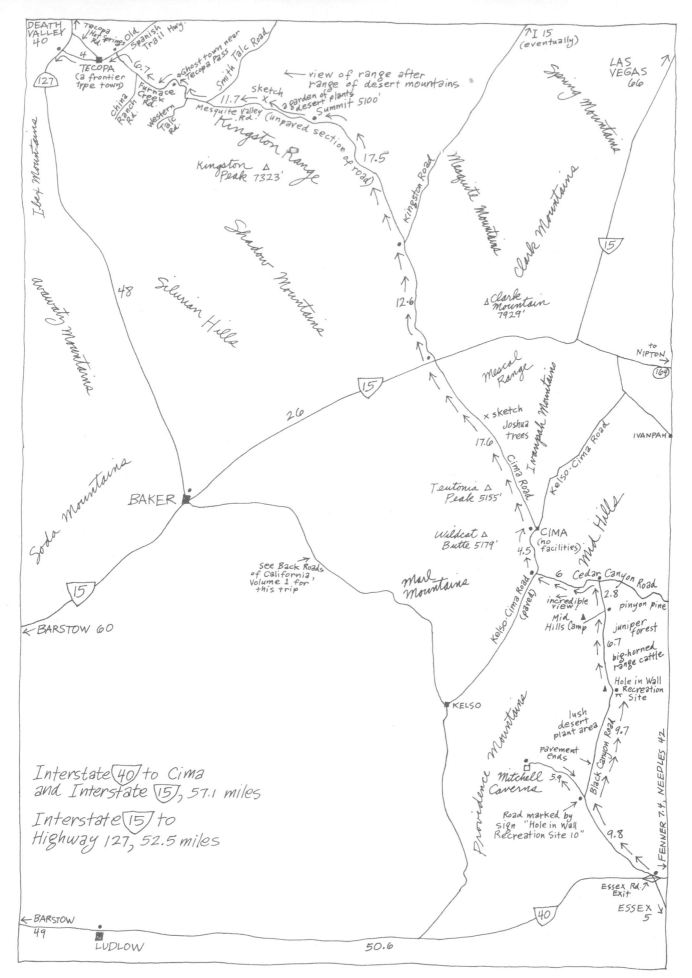

DEATH VALLEY 40

Tecopa Hot Springs Rd.

Old Spanish Trail Hwy.

I 15 (eventually)

LAS VEGAS 66

127

4

TECOPA (a frontier type town)

6.7

Ghost town near Tecopa Pass

Smith Talc Road

view of range after range of desert mountains

Spring Mountains

China Ranch Rd.

Furnace Creek Rd.

western Talc Rd.

11.7

sketch

X a garden of desert plants

Summit 5100'

Mesquite Valley (unpaved section of road)

Kingston Range

17.5

Kingston Road

Mesquite Mountains

Clark Mountains

15

Ibex Mountains

Kingston Peak 7323' △

Shadow Mountains

12.6

△ Clark Mountain 7929'

to NIPTON 164

Avawatz Mountains

48

Silurian Hills

15

26

Mescal Range

Ivanpah Mountains

x sketch Joshua trees

17.6

Cima Road

Kelso-Cima Road

IVANPAH

Soda Mountains

Teutonia △ Peak 5155'

BAKER

Wildcat △ Butte 5179'

CIMA (no facilities)

4.5

Mid Hills

15

See Back Roads of California, Volume 1 for this trip

Marl Mountains

Kelso-Cima Road (paved)

6

Cedar Canyon Road

2.8

pinyon pine

BARSTOW 60

incredible view!

Mid Hills Camp

juniper forest

6.7

big-horned range cattle

KELSO

Providence Mountains

Hole in Wall Recreation Site

9.7

lush desert plant area

Black Canyon Road

FENNER 7.4, NEEDLES 42

Interstate 40 to Cima and Interstate 15, 57.1 miles

Interstate 15 to Highway 127, 52.5 miles

pavement ends

Mitchell Caverns 5.9

Road marked by sign "Hole in Wall Recreation Site 10"

9.8

Essex Rd. Exit

ESSEX 5

BARSTOW 49

LUDLOW

40

50.6

Joshua trees
near Cima,
San Bernardino
County

Excelsior Mine Road
(map, page 186)
There is a good view of
the Kingston Range as
I approach the summit.
At 5,100 feet, I pass
through a region of heavy
mining activity. At one
point I wend my way
through mine tailings.

Barrel cactus and cholla,
near Tecopa Pass,
San Bernardino County

I notice garden-like arrangements of cactus and other desert plants growing on the rocky mountainside and choose barrel cactus and cholla to draw.

The road from here descends into a vast desert valley. I pass a ghost town at Tacopa Pass and later pass the frontier-like town of Tacopa before reaching Highway 127.

Epilogue

Picturesque, old-fashioned back roads are in danger of disappearing entirely. They are threatened even in remote and sparsely populated areas of the United States. Like paths, these roads once followed the contours of the land. In fact, many of the roads followed early Indian and pioneer trails.

Today massive machines carve and redistribute the earth to achieve as direct and straight a route as possible. We have all seen road-cuts along our speed-oriented highways. They look to me like ugly wounds that have been inflicted upon the earth. I agree that we must have high-speed freeways and secondary roads; what I object to is the road-building philosophy that _all_ roads are candidates for reconstruction. And from a practical standpoint (as a taxpayer), I am concerned about the increasing costs of road building and maintenance, as more and more widening, cutting, and paving takes place. It is possible that, in many instances, grading the gravel and dirt roads and smoothing the asphalt ones are all that is really necessary.

I don't believe that a straight road is necessarily a safe one. It seems to me that a direct route encourages speed and thus increases the potential for danger.

Arriving at the destination has always been only part of my purpose. It is equally important to me to enjoy the journey itself. (It is _my_ life that is passing by, and I do not wish to waste it peering at freeway asphalt, cars, trucks, and recreational vehicles.)

The price we pay for speed is too high. I feel it is time to slow down, or at least not to increase the pace, especially on back roads.

I have investigated and catalogued back roads in eleven states. My travels have been exhilarating and have given me a great deal of joy. They have left me with a profound concern for the future of the beautiful back roads of America.

Index

Page numbers in italics indicate maps.

Graffiti, Donner Lake Road, Nevada County

Note: Anyone noticing discrepancies in the maps
or anyone aware of further changes is encouraged
to write to the author at:

19210 Highway 128,
Calistoga, California
94515

Materials used by the author
for the making of this book
were smooth- or rough-surfaced
Fabriano watercolor paper,
rapidograph 00 pen with
Osmiroid ink, bamboo pen
with India ink, Winsor &
Newton series 233 brushes
and Grumbacher 4701
Erminette brushes.

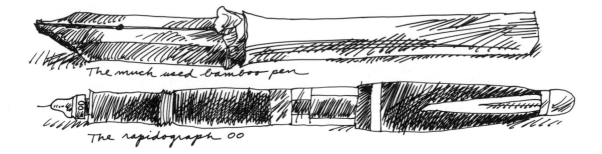

The much used bamboo pen

The rapidograph 00

Historic Spots in California,
published by Stanford University
Press, was of great help in
the author's research.

Book design, drawings, maps,
and calligraphy by Earl Thollander